BNP

OTHER EDITIONS IN THIS SERIES

About *Best New Poets*

————————

Welcome to *Best New Poets 2019*, our fifteenth annual anthology of fifty poems from emerging writers. In *Best New Poets*, the term "emerging writer" is defined narrowly: we restrict our anthology to poets who have yet to publish a book-length collection of poetry. Our goal is to provide special encouragement and recognition to poets just starting in their careers, the many writing programs they attend, and the magazines that publish their work.

From February to May of 2019, *Best New Poets* accepted nominations from writing programs and magazines in the United States and Canada. Each magazine and program could nominate two writers, and those poets could send a free submission to the anthology. For a small entry fee, writers who had not received nominations could also submit poems as part of our open competition. Eligible poems were either published after January 1, 2018, or unpublished. Which means you are not only reading new poets in this book, but also some of their most recent work.

In all, we received over 2,000 submissions for a total of roughly 3,750 poems. A pool of readers and the series editor ranked these submissions, sending a few hundred selections to this year's guest editor, Cate Marvin, who chose the final fifty poems that appear here.

Contents

Best
NEW
Poets

2019

50 Poems from Emerging Writers

Guest Editor Cate Marvin

Series Editor Jeb Livingood

This book is published in cooperation with *Meridian* (readmeridian.org) and the University of Virginia Press (upress.virginia.edu).

For additional information, visit us at
bestnewpoets.org
twitter.com/BestNewPoets
facebook.com/BestNewPoets

Cover and interior design elements originally by Atomicdust | atomicdust.com

Cover images from Crestock

Text set in Adobe Garamond Pro and Bodoni

Printed by Sheridan Books, Inc.

ISBN: 978-0-9975623-3-0
ISSN: 1554-7019

Margaret Cipriano
Home Alone

While the husband is at work, I fold napkins
into neat squares. Handsome men knock on my door,
they want to show me their books, but are distracted
by my bright, honest napkins. I tell them I'm sorry,
I can't help them helping me. They say not to worry,
they're more interested in my pink azaleas. Those *are*
azaleas? No, I tell them. That's a child's drawing. The house moves
in the breeze. The whole thing
is starting to feel a little flimsy. What about
the rooms? They ask. These aren't rooms, I reply,
those are the pink azaleas. Your husband must be
a physicist, they say. They don't know
but the husband defeathers magpies. I match corner
to corner. One of the men pulls out a small knife
and begins slicing an orange. Where did you get that orange? I ask.
The little jeweled wedges. This isn't an orange, he says,
it's the name of the boy who loves you. He holds up the peel.
A smile with no teeth.

—Nominated by The Ohio State University
MFA Program in Creative Writing

Rachael Uwada Clifford
Boys by Shape

I want more of everything. Octopuses have three hearts.
Are you happy with the way things are? I asked you.
What I really wanted to ask was, *What would you do*
with three hearts? You had just come in from the rain,
your clothes carrying sky. I was in the kitchen, breaking
the wooden moon out of an avocado. I wanted
to learn you by shape, I was looking for
a wideness, the hollers, the ways
you sprawled and gave. I wanted to be able
to see it even in late light, to feel it
in the wild-limbed dark. I liked you
because I didn't have to think or be
honest, so much. Like when you go
to the grocery store and buy things you can't
really live off of: dark chocolate, cheap wine,
cinnamon, pounds of oranges, pulpy black fruit.
It was a kind of paring down, being
with you—a winnowing to the wingbone.
I don't think this is going anywhere, I said, and
I didn't know where it was supposed to
go—it is just a thing you say
when you mean to say
that you have been starving.

Annie Virginia
The Teenage Girls Calling Me Back from the Dead Will Say

Come back tipsier, come back remembering
the dreams you tried to follow from sleep
but their lights went out.

Come back a person
never born of your mother.
You'll look like city pool water
with the floating legs of strangers,
looking clean until you run your hands through it
and they come up willowed with hairs.
Maybe still sterile. We just want to see
you see how her absence looks on you.

Come back without lockjaw.
We mean lighten the fuck up.
You're cool, right?

Come back and cause car wrecks
for the boys who have convinced us
the taste of licorice is kind, and we'll make
an urban legend of you, wear your face
on our t-shirts like a background to solo cups, light
candles of shrines to you
in our rooms where we take the others.

As children, we waited for the tailor
and stuck clothespins into the first layer of our skin,
looked at one thousand of ourselves in fitting room

mirrors, imagined if it was us
who killed the cardinal in the driveway.

Come back and say we will be saints one day.

Come back and tell us not to shower after it happens,
wait while doctors scrape the wet ashes into doggie bags.

Come back and confirm there are enough ashes
to build a god from, one that no one believes.

Come back and murder our mothers,
come back and make our mothers pretty
again, at least crack the frames of the photos
of how they looked before us.

On weekends, we plan for our future
by watching our fathers' old football tapes.
When we found the skulls under our brothers' beds,
we were good, and hid them deeper.
You must know.

Come back so you can tell us if it's true
what we heard shaking in the dark,
why it felt like we'd heard it before
years from now and if it means we are
what came from your fingers, your bile,
and the brazen flood between your legs.
If it's true, we're telling everyone.
If it's true, we'll dig you up
when the birds chirping before dawn
won't stop and it feels like we have missed
a funeral, an important one, and we think

pulling our teeth from our heads
will be enough to make up for it
and we need you, we'll need you then.
Come with a story of how asking
can be answered.

Maya Marshall
[midnight with a new moon]

what do I know about being black
but my mother's hand and mine

but my sister's back in her white white wedding dress
(her newly widowed face under new white hair)

but my brother's black boy feet running running
against the NES power pad

(didn't know what was chasing him)
I knew it meant dad

would visit and the boys would be boys
the finger's narrow escape from fire-

crackers mommy in the night with fire-
flies I caught

my black meant country club
kids got out of the pool and I didn't notice until years later

but what do I know
may as well be white

except my grandmother washed white
women's floors and was common poor

except *shawty what yo name is?* and *you talk white, you stuck up bitch*
what do I know about black

but my obese african-american woman fibroids
or the policeman's gun to my face

the black policewoman, saying
but what you really gon' be college girl?

or a white man who loves me and is
noticing my *blackness a lot less lately*

or another black woman trying to check me
on any given day in my grown ass life

girl don't
you say: *oh, she's basically white*

and I know you're worried
we can't both exist

in some rooms, you know,
even the fact of the conversation is treason

2.
[well bottom] [a shadow] [anansi] [hottentot berry baker jackson] [nostrils]
[hearted] [coal] [lips] [2 million American prisoners] [Baldwin Lorde
hooks Morrison] [lung] [lives matter] [enuf for ya?]

—Nominated by *Muzzle Magazine*

Parker Hobson
Field Notes: Class Treasurer (Former)

Every demon has a fatal weakness, we were told in Scripture class.
Ever since, I've kept careful spiral

notebooks of possible clues: how the morning split
creeklight through her antique curtains. How *on earth*

as it is in heaven. How across cultures, old men
all sneak up theatrically to flick each other's ears.

How the Rouse's cashier sighed "baby,
what're you doing drinking Schlitz." How the *satori*

of sliding off wet shorts. How the *satori* of sliding
off her shorts. How standing too fast, you forget

your name for a second. How *He will come to judge the quick.*

Still, I've never quite figured out how to serif
all these sunless Sam's Club sunsets

into battle plans. I was too flatfooted to rollerblade
like the cul-de-sac heroes from afterschool cable, so I'd clomp

home in kneepads I didn't need. And I only mention that
to mention this: I can't strip the past

from this place. Everything I'm trying to say

is the ghost-bike, chained white, at Piety & St. Claude.
is the grocery lobsters floating, claws bound, and Lou Rawls comes on.
is every couples' skate that's ever been watched from a too-bright snack bar—

is in my brother's old coat and basketball shorts and
my ride's not coming.

Charlie Peck
Noise

I once attended a stand-up show in Amsterdam,
      and not speaking a word of Dutch I just laughed
   along with the crowd, letting myself get caught
up with the noise. It's the same logic of applause
      and food fights. I can't think about the bubonic
   plague without getting anxious. When I watch

Planet Earth, I root for both prey and predator.
      The border between humor and disgust blurs
   neatly so it's often hard to say. I was driving
home from the grocery store last week
      and saw that my neighbor had painted and hung
   a new sign on his shed: THEEVES WILL BE SHOT

and Kate asked, *Who's Theeves?* In high school
      a boy did a Gallagher impression after prom,
   smashing watermelons on stage with a hammer,
his fake mustache falling off mid-swing,
      and then two weeks later his parents received a bill
   for $30,000 to replace the pulp-smattered curtain.

Or that time in second grade after we had
      just moved when a quiet boy in my class asked
   for a ride home. My mother, new to the city,
got lost, and cross-stitched neighborhoods
      in the fading light because the boy didn't know
   which was his, and he started crying, and my mother

started to cry too, and we drove until the boy saw
        a familiar park, and eventually we found it,
    his house, and his mother was on the lawn
with two officers, and she's crying, too,
        and then the drive home after, my mother
    whispering *Shit, Shit, Shit,* and wiping her eyes.

        —Nominated by *Quarterly West*

Joy Priest
American Honey

It's easier than you thought—leaving.
Only one night spent sleeping on your own
in a motel parking lot beneath the stars
of a summer Okolona. Your long-built dread
dispersing like gas into a brilliantly Black
Appalachian sky. For once, you are a girl

unmolested. You could do this: be a girl
without a home. Always gone. Perpetually leaving
behind Strip Mall, U.S.A. & the dark
green dumpster you raid for food, something to own
& the two kids no one will take care of, the dread
that comes on when their father squeezes your ass. Sparkle,

let your freedom build slow like the death of a star
across the years. & when she calls for you—granddaughter
of Elvis, confederate flag bikini, voice you dread—
let the interstate's roar swallow her sound. In your leaving
you see the country for the first time. Your very own
seeing. When he howls for you, your body is a silent, Black

barn hidden in wild grass & your locs—pastoral, Black—
are ropes for him, swaying from its rafters. Dangling stars.
It's easier than you imagined—leaving behind your own
mother. Her daughter, her ghost. But now you can be a girl
on a back patio with three white men & you can leave
with their money, egg suede cowboy hat adorning your dreads.

You've swallowed the Mezcal worm of your fear.
Now you're standing in the cowboy's convertible, Black
wind at the edge of the camera's frame. You're leaving
with the get-away boy you found sparking
in a K-mart parking lot. You're keeping it alive—your girlhood,
the adrenaline, the novelty, the dying star that you own

a million miles away. You're learning how to own
yourself, how to be 14-deep in a 12-seater without dread,
how to disarm, how to let it go when the white girl
from Florida says nigga again, how to be the only Black
girl among strangers. Dancing around a bonfire under the stars.
Singing out of the sunroof down the interstate. Leaving

each new town you meet and own a memory in. Leaving
behind your mother's dread-veined eyes. Fuseless stars.
Learn it all, girl, until what you've left behind is a brilliant Black.

Gen Del Raye
Litmus Test

In high school in Kobe, the test
was simple.

We sang part of a song
from a TV show

and waited for you
to fill in the rest.

The part we sang
was always the same.

If need be, you could
learn it.

Now I live in California
not far from a place

where a painter woke to bullet-cracked glass
in 1942. I live near a place

where a dormitory stood
for Japanese-Americans

refused a room
by everyone else.

Back then, the test
was called *one drop*

which was, I am told
not an actual drop

but one-sixteenth of a bloodline
or a third of a liter

of foreignness.

There were many things back then
that didn't mean the same thing

as the words that were used
to say them.

Like the place in the camps
for mixed blood orphans

they called
the Children's Village.

Or the graveyard in Yokohama
mainly for children

abandoned or aborted by Japanese mothers
and callous or dishonest

or dead or desperate or simply realistic
American fathers

and this graveyard which is squeezed
between train tracks and the dirt

of two public schools
holding bodies that belong by blood

and by statute to two different countries
is known as the Negishi

Foreigner's Cemetery.

I tell you there is
a whole world of tests:

the dog that couldn't
be with me in a room

because it suffered at the hands
of Asians, someone said

the boy who yelled that I was the one
who bombed Pearl Harbor.

My father's test
which he explained the day

he bought me a globe
is the one I like best.

You find the places
your parents were born in

and all the places
you've ever lived

and take the average
which usually lands you

somewhere in a sweep
of ocean.

—Nominated by *Up North Lit*

Meriwether Clarke
Follow the Leader

Someone once told me girls
who develop too soon are like dolphins—
always wet and speaking in tongues
no one understands. Their breasts

learn early, though, they are not
like fins. There is no underwater
flight for things the shape of little earths.
There is only digging by mouths

that smell of damp grass
and water that makes you float
face down. It is no surprise it's hard
to trust men who want

to touch me. In dreams I burn comic books and
renaissance paintings, anything with women
the shape of finely tuned guitars. In real life
I lunge across my bedroom to tighten

my thighs. I trace figure eights
on car windows. I wear
braids coiled
around a milk-clear gaze.

Jihyun Yun
Menstruation Triptych

I.

Happy to be bleeding,
I fold the unused
test into the black hem
of my pocket just to carry
this solitude with me.
Seedless belly, beloved
fallow, I.

Happy to be bleeding,
I treat myself to sangria
and ice cream, weave
flowers of invasive
species in my hair,
sing praises to Korean
over-the-counter BC.

At home, I'm so happy
to be bleeding, I pummel
my stomach against
the kitchen counter,
just in case. I know
it doesn't work
that way, but he came without
permission and inside.
I'm irrational is what I mean.

Bloodless, others fly
to nearby countries to terminate
but I'm too woman, too poor.

Lord, in this life I'll happily
bleed and bleed. Let the
animals gnaw through every
door. Let the tides overpower.

II.

She's never wanted to mother though the world's demanded from her
nothing else. She holds the napkin to her girlhood, watches the cerise
leech into the quilted fabric. Thank heavens for periods, the rivers
they carve into their beds of mortal meat. Tissue blossoms. Blood tea.
Thirteen, she is my mother, thinking of the fabled student, years ago,
who was never taught menstruation. Who thought the red escaping
her human aperture was a sign of deadly sickness, wrote a letter to her
mother, and took her own life. *Forgive me Mama, I don't want to die
slowly. I'm sorry. I'm sorry.* In a world of men, this is the cost of blood.
Why let girls bleed without telling them what it means? Why bloody
your hands on another's blood-body journey? She wraps the cloth
close to her blood-body, draining the day closed. She thinks, *Praise
this act of escaping,* even though it is her own womanly heat escaped.
Please live freely in this blood vine of your singular life. In time, I
will lodge myself within you and halt the cycle, the napkin still white
between your thighs. I know I will not be worth it, but somewhere, it
is written. Beloved, was I selfish to come merely as I am?

III.

Here, it is not my cycle that bleeds
me, but my lover tearing through
before I am ready. It should have
mattered when he didn't care
about my pain, but in love,
I love even the wounds.
Evening primrose open
beyond the window, lifting
their stamens towards the night.

I understand.
The organic green tangle I am
also blooms best under moonlight.
Six moons from now, I won't be here
anymore. I'll be in New York scalding
my tongue on diner coffee, spitting
the grinds on my plate of eggs scraped
immaculate. I'll be drunk and happy
on 32nd street. I'll be twenty-three,
I'll finally understand all he did to me

on that blue bed. Gondolas
rocking to driftwood in my dreams.
The hurt he said I was born to eat.
My, *Stop.* And then my, *Yes.*
I bleed like girls are taught to bleed,
pretending I am fine. *I tore you
badly*, he says with pride.
He holds his reddened fingers
to my eyes to show me
what I'm made of.

—Nominated by *Blue Mesa Review*

Noah Davis
Short-Haired Girl's Father Confesses Her Conception

After my wife and I laid in a turned field with the waxing moon watching, after I boiled nettles and served them with her cornbread, after I made her bloodroot tea sweetened with red clover, I knew I was too weak to reach where flesh is spun, cord by cord until heat and breath are one.

I visited Witch James at the confluence of Bucks and Kettle Run.

He crushed the fruit of devil's walking stick, combined it with birch bark and asked if I could smell milk or dirt.

When I said *well water,* he spat.

I paid him chicken livers and a mule's hoof for the shaved ginseng.

It won't make the bobcat's pecker taste better, but it'll help get yours up.

I waited at the bottom of a draw where I'd seen the bobcat cross the trickle of a spring.

I didn't like to hunt at night.

When I was a child, Pa said animals didn't have souls, but behind his back, Ma shook her head.

I feared that once I unbound the spirit from the body it might have trouble seeing in the dark and come barreling into me.

The bullet curled the tom, who in death did not drop the rabbit, and I left her in his mouth while I removed his member.

His penis turned over the fire like rotting stinkhorn.

I ate it in the woods.

I waited there, as I do after killing, to see if what I'd taken would stay down.

Patrick James Errington
Fieldwork in Secret

All day in the heat they would talk. Some sang
even, though no one could hear the others'
words through the grit and noise, the rusted
grind of machinery. But still they'd drive their
voices like fenceposts into the hard din of it,
not for a fence for keeping in some untamed
thing, but rather just the plain act of keeping.
As a boy, I used to cross the fields to watch
them at it, the sweat, their mouths moving as
practiced as their hands, shaping the steel dust,
the air—into what, I could never quite say.
A craft of some sort, of sound, of stale light.
Whenever my father came home he'd leave
the keys dangling in the pickup, a scum of grey
around the bath and, every now and then, her
(my mother, I mean), driving with me away
for days, weeks even, but we always came and
were taken back. I guess he liked the act of it,
leaving. I still remember him mumbling along
to the radio, but at home he never sang, not
to anyone, barely spoke in more than those
sentences he set out on the table, cruel little
heirlooms. My mother who spoke enough
for all of us told me how she eventually had
to ask him to stop saying he loved her, and so
he did, though as he neared the end she'd hear
him at night muttering the words and her name
over and over as though they were a kind of

work he'd done all his life and now his breath,
like his hands, was set to it. I could always tell
as he and I drove back that we were almost home
when, though we kept no cattle, no horses,
the untended fields were scored with fences.

Shannon Sankey
Lonesome Errand

& the red moon buoyant & the grocery cart shepherd driving his clanging row back inside & the walk to the car long & our blue bags of canned vegetables spinning in silent circles from our wrists & our time together incalculable, as if it would go on for us, the chips & dip on the dashboard, the KFC bucket turning above our heads, the cemetery on our right & then our left, & inside us, our sticky cells selfsame, our bellies full with the perfect peace of giving up, for today, on getting to know each other, how incessant that work had been, I admit, how exhausted we became with bewilderment, how bored with the pattern of windshield rain on the face of the other, cold cast of a streetlight on the face of the other. & we wasted it like water some nights, we carried on as if there would be no lonesome errand, no next lives for us, my mother & me, though she knew the truth & said nothing.

Katherine Fallon
Letters from the Farm

I

Catbird at the window. Black capped, unexpected
this far west. I'd never have recognized it but for its crying

mimicry: sounds like, sounds like, isn't. You didn't tell me
they nest near ground. Little potential to plummet and vulnerable,

like an anthill, to the footstep. Longer now since you loved me
than you loved me, the difference stretches narrowly on, deepens.

Emptiness bright as beak shine.
Expectation's tight cup, loose dirt: a home.

II

This week in the city where we met, a woman was strangled
with her bra and left just where, just how she fell. I hear nothing

from you. That girl who lassoed you like a calf kept you like one:
quartered. You stayed close, devoted, hid your pretty throat

from me as though I'd been the blind and careless one. We were
given a chance to love, so I did. You wouldn't know a gift even if.

III

At noon, a little girl was swept into the canal behind me like
so much dirt beneath a rug, her body a secret the baffles will keep.

I heard the sirens but knelt, back turned, willingly unaware.
You can't imagine my grief.

I'd been winnowing the greening down to what might grow
tall and wanted. I had just learned to be happy.

IV

In the field where bone became stone long before I knew you,
a flock of sparrows sits quiet as quartz between plumed grasses.

My footsteps disturb them into a swarm (mine only;
yours withdrawn). Startled by small birds I've startled,

I stand still and let my loss set in: the heart slows,
the hands unfurl to cup the air, in petition.

V

What of the mustard tucked into a bed of cauliflower,
or the magpie's dive-bomb wingspan, fanned across

the rim rock? My boot leaks, sticks fast into the over-
watered field, and I know I was mistaken: none

of my new learning is intended for you. I approach
the land I keep alone and like a storm, hand raised

above the brow to see, far off, what's coming.

Megan J. Arlett
Jaw

The baby cries
so I put him in the cupboard like a biology experiment,
take meticulous notes

about sunlight and soil. He babbles
in the dark. I scribble sounds
on a notepad: looping, doughy drawings, words

not yet words. I call him *sweetpea*
through the door because the literature says
this is how to raise a gentle son.

Little lamb in his dark casket.
Little muffled timebomb.
Tears and rain, tears and rain.

The smallest dog in the house barks at the bathtub
all month long. I too
have watched a possum family

trundle out from the crawl space across the lawn.
I know they live in the vacancy
beneath my naked, bathing body.

What does a mother possum call her babies?
Should I clasp mine
in my mouth

to keep his feet from puddles,
his mind safe from filth.
Or carry him

through the world on my back
hoping
one day a woman like me—

her dress catching on the wind, arms pregnant
with a paper bag filled to the lip
by oranges—

won't have to call him
dog, hoping he'll never howl at her
down the street.

—Nominated by University of North Texas Creative Writing

James Davis
In Houston

Remembering it is like remembering the womb.
The heat. The concrete. The tofu sandwiches.

I was democratic there. I had directions in three languages.
I was punched in a Fiesta Mart parking lot. I was rigged.

I made out with hipsters, some of them straight,
all of them strangers, at a Seventies sportswear party.

Later, one told me, "You're right, MySpace
is for fascists and faggots, of which you are both."

I dabbled in Montrose and Montaigne, snorted half a line
behind the dumpster behind Texas Art Supply.

My French professor complimented my nasals.
Saint Barthélemy, she helped me say. *Sandbar tail me.*

There were the minor drugs: Adderall, cowboy killers, ironic
Tab. I was a sanctimonious double major. I learned

how things went bad. Potatoes liquefied in my pantry.
During the library renovations, I snuck classmates

up to the empty eighth floor and fingered their assholes.
How juvenile, my quest for omniscience.

Kemi Alabi

Soft & Beautiful Just For Me Relaxer, No-Lye Conditioning Creme, Children's Regular

DIRECTIONS

Snatch the could-be-girl-'cept-she-too-dark
-'cept-them-nigga-naps child by the braids.

Slice them open. Rake the comb through.
Cue the scalp pop, the scab-robed choir.

Teach the tribe dirge: staccato rip-rip
crescendo into sizzle and shred.

Litter the neck with butchered kinks,
a gutter-fur shawl, diseased offering.

Heat stroke, swamp drown, chemical spill,
decompose, exorcise, drag and prop

until brillo collapses, satin rises,
arabesques and curtsies with a snap.

Heaven's darkest halo is a high yellow.
On earth, at last, a crown is cast in black.

INGREDIENTS

Propylene Glycol (Antifreeze)
These winters, nothing natural survives.

Helianthus Annuus (Sunflower)
Half the native wildlife, extinct.

Hydroxyethylcellulose (KY Jelly)
The rest, tweaked to triple their bloom.

Citronellol (Repellent)
Teach her to burn

Salvia Officinalis (Sage)
All smoke, no fire.

Aqua (Water)
Refuse to call god by name.

WARNING

A child is made of water. A Black girl,
open flame. Product may catch fire.

Osun may wrestle from her kitchen,
snap your comb in two.

There may be no Black girls,
only burning gods.

There may be no Jesus,
just empire.

You may be both the army
and the scorched earth below.

DIRECTIONS

What was the Atlantic
before it became
a graveyard?

Before crops meant
auction blocks,

which dance brought
the rain?

For best results,
cover her. Fall
in praise.

Be cloudthick
and unpartable.

Be tangled,
skystuck waves.

Robin Gow
rice & rain

all the rain came down at once like a dropped bag
of aquarium pebbles. too much for the street to swallow:
all gravel & grit. i feel the saltwater rushing
in my mouth as i hit the shore—sand becoming rice.
the pot on the stove—put on the lid. we read the
back of the bag—bring the water to a boil—it
protests in the clouds. rainwater peeling open
car windows to fill the floor—make mobile your
lakes & the herons will come—don't feed the birds rice.
my favorite summer storms are the ones
that come too fast. they remind me so much of myself:
gathering their gray hair in a bouquet to beat
against the highway. i think of the times the thunder
would toss geodes at the street until they cracked open,
about dad telling my brother & i to go upstairs
& shut the windows before the storm snuck inside.
the car prayed until it drove on water—ocean barreling
toward us like a great big whale: blueness open & mouth full
of salt. you ask if we should stir the rice & the water
hisses & spits. we often forget about the ghosts
who kneel in pots of water. there's always a wooden spoon. i keep
mine in the glove box. taking it out, i park the car with
the four-ways on. other monsters slosh past.
we get out on the side of the road. kneeling i plunge
the spoon into the bank: chicken broth & rice.
rain warming our bodies until there's no
mistaking us from the stove. i burn my feet getting
back into the car. our flesh turns chicken-white & tender.

somewhere in all of this i managed
to drive across the whole unknown ocean—the one
without a name that shows up only when it downpours.
makes tides that eat radar & sailors.
picks rice grains from her teeth.
the other side is not land, but soft rice steaming
& ready. our legs sink in. take a spoonful of me
before i drive home a second time. the sun emerging like
a quartered bell pepper. i'm thinking of
lying in a rain puddle with you & falling apart
into a palm full of cooked rice.

—Nominated by *Poetry*

M.K. Foster
Aubade with Dolly Parton on Vinyl

—if I build a house of you in spring, if I want to watch you
flood with *light wood ash smoke,* if we've been in bed long enough
to open, if I open, if I let you open me, if I open myself opening
you, if I break a part of you open, if I nail my bones to yours, *if
I should stay,* if I kiss *knee elbow wrist,* if your head against my ribs,
if my arms collapsed around you, if it costs me to keep you (what
costs a body), if you are my last prayer, my favorite prayer, my only
prayer, my one phone call with the worst words in the worst order,
if you are the beautiful cracks in the windshield only I can see (even
if you aren't), if we've been in bed too long, my dearest, if you are
my darling, if I'm your deer, if you hit me with your car, if I'm caught
in your windshield, if it's all my fault, if it's Tuesday and you love
Tuesdays, *if I should stay,* if I want you in the worst way, if I am weighed
and found wanting, if I'm full of shit (so are you), if I burn for this,
if I am burning, if my heart could burn a house down, if I'm always
burning down the wrong house (you), if your face like glass apples,
if your skin like a rosy room packed with sleeping pickled animals,
if your eyes like fire-poker holes, like small idiot stars blistering
the black-out curtains this morning, if freckles of light like toxic petals
of ivory mold speckling the sagging ceiling, if we've been in bed too
long (how long is too long), if we fucked, if we're fucked, if we fucked up,
if we couldn't help ourselves, if we're helpless, if I suck (so do you),
if you're useless as a glass axe or wet matches (even if you aren't),
if I'm a goner without you, *O my darling* (and I am), *sweetheart,*
if I'm the punchline of every country western song, *if I should stay,*
if *I would only be in your way,* if *I Will Always Love You* is always
playing somehow, somewhere always crooning the same tune
on-loop, if this is hell (this feels like hell), if I'd follow you to hell,

if you holding on to me for dear life, my dear, is hell, if I feel like hell
for what's happened, if this is hell (this bed), if hell is a bed (this bed),
if we've been in bed too long (too long is too long), if it kills us dead
in the end (what costs a body in the end), if I pay in *light wood ash smoke*
like this is the last time, if this is the last time, even if we know what
comes next (we know what comes next), if the cherry tree like a chest
x-ray breaking up the window white with dark bones, if your face like
a grubby water glass waiting for rain, if your eyes like dug-up graves,
if your eyes in this light eaten out by light, sockets hollow as moon
craters hollow as us (*if us*), *if us*, if heavy husks of marbled dust

—Nominated by *The Account*

Molly Bess Rector
Self-Portrait as Nuclear Fallout

I.

Mornings I rise
      a few degrees at a time
and dress myself
      beside the water
in silence, brush iodine
      into my hair, adorn
my cheeks in excess
      moth wings, place
on my clavicle
      a broach: a six-legged frog.

II.

A lot of men come to study
      my body.
They gather
      impossible data:
What was it bore me
out of (their) control?
Back, they slide:
      May hunker?
May take shelter?
      Too late.

I'm building a realm
      on reactions.

III.

I bet you'd never guess
        how still the cooling pool
when once: tsunami,
          sudden power surge, flood—
all this a kind of coronation
        for the queen whose unstable
diadem slips between
        her eyes, radiates.

Even the dust I slough
        glows.

IV.

These men
        look for origins.
Origin:
        when we're born
the universe spins one way;
          when we die
it spins the other—
           procedure for the spirit
to follow.
        Does anyone still
          follow procedures?
Or think we can forestall
            the end
with a good plan?

V.

I've never learned to think
except by acting. A different kind
                of doctrine.

Granted: how fragile the core.
Granted: all systems rupture
                when shaken hard

enough, given the chance
                to melt down.

VI.

Origin: even that man came
emergently.
                Wild alert, the ambulance squall;

his mother's howls a kind of sonic fallout—
                his refusal to be contained. Sure—

he can call me disaster if he wants.

Why does it matter
                                whose fault
I am? Now
                        I've made
this gown of waste.

Luc Diggle
Plum Wine

I learned how to make plum wine
from Etsuko Tanaka.

She was born on the edge of Tokyo
as World War II ended in its atomic flash

and grew up pickling radishes
between rocks along the Tsurumi river.

It's simple: potato spirits and rock sugar
laced between layers of sour plums.

The fruits never ripen. They can't
withstand the early summer storms

and so are consigned to wine and pickles.
It's not uncommon to see them scattered

beneath a bony plum tree, rotting back into the loam;
headstones of a season we'll never sip.

Aidan Ryan
That's Not the Way It Feels

I didn't see it so much as feel the cold
when you put out all the watch fires in your gestures
but I did see you hadn't watched a single one
of my stories since the morning before the morning
before I left you and is that petty? It's Borderline,
by Madonna, and I don't notice the song despite
the quietly brutal B Minor of the pre-chorus
because I'm looking for an outlet and thinking about
how the constant howl in Heathrow reminds me
of your breath, the way it cuts
over the all-season hush of the vents in my apartment
I only hear it when Madonna's icy voice says *Something*
in your eyes is making such a fool of me
I wonder whether my memories are more or less yours
and I don't feel distant from you, but I do
notice the heartbeat's interstices in turbulence
and want to be rocked either to blister
and ash somewhere
over Newfoundland and Labrador
or to sleep in the basket that you make with your limbs
I don't feel distant, but I do wonder what we said
last week, when we made an empty bench
into a private Ithaca and were a family there, and how
did we come to this performance
sending push notifications like ferocious air
kisses, starting trash fires in each other's
wishlists and hurt-curating mixtapes across
the galaxy of our Friend Activity, like

If you want me let me know
and I want you
to see that I'm listening
to Jim Croce's Operator, and asking Alexa
to place a call, as if one day
she'll pronounce your name correctly, perfectly,
like a magic eight-ball's blue die suddenly
opening a new face up to the murky window
and reassuring me that regular, healthy people
sometimes drink alone—I once
asked an empty bathroom Does anybody
yearn anymore? do you feel yearned? or only
needed? I yearn you to retweet
the scared anger out of me, like kissing a snake
bite *But that's not the way it feels*
I ask you if every poem begins
with feeling you think I mean received but I mean
choice you tell me every poem starts off as a comeback
you mean retort I thought you meant return
the podcast between us says
that human saliva contains a painkiller, opiorphin
six times more powerful than morphine and
all my poems end up as shitty podcasts
let me tell you a true story
about tomorrow when we were apex
consumers in the supermarket
olive bar making a language out of tapenade
and artichokes and being broke and brokenness
and fluency was morning after morning after
showering when you would press your
skincare to my skincare and our borderlines
were arbitrary liplines like a thalweg
(is a word I learned from Dictionary

waiting to see your curls in Bulk
and Imports it is the ever-changing and locationless
exact middle of a waterway between two states) I lose
your touch like a territory, everybody's fault, a feeling
there is nothing on the outside of my nothing, I am
wave-tossed away from you, across the room
or further and the only coming back is a half-
measure toward the middle of whatever home
is knowing I could tell you
that whenever Madonna's Borderline comes on
a speaker in any ceiling anywhere I'll forever
bring your hands to the bruised face in my mind's
intercontinental morning darkness where
the seatback screens reveal us
to be chasing, even gaining on the sun
like finally the cats got control of the flashlight
I switch on my personal heaven
and read about *a love that's proved*
by steady gazing / Not at each other
but in the same direction
and on this plane at least we
all gaze in the same direction
so, I guess, we all must be living proof
of some kind of love, and I believe
in an alternative to knowing
and wonder if you're lying
on your right side or your left
as you let yourself be chased
and caught by the star-sign
that I'm chasing, I wonder
if you know that in the pocket
of your elbows and your knees

I am there
that I am one thing
and it is yours

Keith Kopka

For a Moment I Feel Immortal, or, Rather, Disappointed

No matter what the graffiti on this wall
tells me, I'm positive that Chey

and Rich will not be *2gether*
4ever. But we learn

so much about death when
we're young, its spring held

taut by the suction
of a popup toy, the shock

when it jumps, despite
our anticipation.

When I was six, I held my breath
in the shower and listened

to my mother run the vacuum
until my body collapsed in the tub basin.

I woke in her arms so confident
of my death that when she'd settled me

with a pillow on the couch and returned to work,
I thought, this must be heaven, watching her

maneuver in large circles around the living room.
Chey and Rich might not even be alive right now,

though they declared this wall
a monument to what they thought they'd be.

When I asked my mom if I could get cookies
in heaven, she looked at me as if something

behind my head were talking. *Go get them yourself,*
she said, *they're right where they've always been.*

Mary Lenoir Bond
Rorschach: I See a Blood Nest

A hose had dispersed your blood
with colossal gusts of water that left
your insides a Rorschach-like
pattern on the ground far below the ledge.

It had been three days, so the red
had turned more brown, slowly baking
on the cement in the hot Sacramento sun.

Your life reduced to a game we played as children,
more like a godly art-kit. *Twirl-o-paint, Magic Spin
Art, Fantastic Spinner.* A lever spun a square
of paper (lives) and paint (love) was poured into the middle.

I found an odd coin with mystical symbols
near the remains. I'm not sure if it was yours
but if it wasn't it's all the more strange. My thumb flipped

the warm metal and it landed just like you, heads. It's dark—
to mention that—I know. It's also unavoidable, carrying this
image along with the coin and a heavy leaf I collected there,
just like every other of life's weighty, sticky sorrows. I was given

the rings from your fingers and a copy of the note,
largely written to me, and then to some of your family,
a couple of friends, and a public *To All Whom* ... address.

It was three months after Kurt's greenhouse death. The two
are forever tied in my mind. I was spared identifying
your body. But many miracles are the nightmares
of others. *So it goes*, a different Kurt said.

The spot where you landed could have
been an opening. The jagged edges to an astral lake.
A portal. A different life and I hope that in this one your uncle

does not infect you. I hope in this life you can swim, float
without falling. A swan. Flightless but graceful, long hook neck,
and committed to a love greater than your own life.
How quickly this life has passed, you'll never know now.

After the funeral, your mother sat curbside, clutching
a big red suitcase, sweating in the 102-degree shadeless sun. *Where
ya going*, we asked, openly clinging to our own bottled liquid escapes.

Mental hospital, she flatly stated. We all nodded, in
a strange sort of unison, immediate with understanding. Somebody
had invited a psychic to the funeral wake. Some people took acid.
Someone said when a body descends from a great height, the soul

leaves the body before landing. Later on, someone who never
even knew you said it was likely very fast and painless, how the neck
tends to just snap. Leaving behind a flightless carcass of bones, flesh,
and perhaps some white feathers as shiny as coins.

Mitchell Jacobs
Chronicle with a Series of Vessels

A deer ate me and shit me out
into peppercorns. I used them
to season my soup. Obviously
I was also the soup. I ate myself
seasoned with myself. Obviously
this is a lie. I was merely the oak
who watched it all happen.

They cut me down. I was heavy
and had such an appealing grain.
I was made into a cabin so quaint
that I moved in. No furniture,
no bed. Oh well. I hung myself
a wooden frame that held a photo
of myself. The man in the photo

is mid-blink. I think I was afraid
to press the shutter at the right time.
All roads from there led back there.
I removed my biological clock
and put it under the floorboards.
My carrots grew. Grizzlies eyed me
hungrily, and I was flattered.

When I died they cremated me
and poured me into a prehistoric urn,
the type of thing I might have crafted
had I been around. The cabin burned.

The picture of me inside burned.
I mixed the ashes into my ashes.
It was all very convenient.

I keep the urn in the credenza
beside the porcelain soup tureen. Now
a giant owl pellet, I arrange my face
of regurgitated hair and bone. A shame
I never managed to meet myself
as myself. Every mirror I see is broken.
No, not cracked. Just plain broken.

—Nominated by *Passages North*

Ösel Jessica Plante

Poem with Duplex Apartment, Mouse, &
a Line by Larry Levis

Our bedroom was windowless, a place where light
went to die, the backyard wild with vine-buckled

chain link, and somewhere behind the refrigerator,
or in the dank beneath the sink, a mouse made

itself familiar with things we did not wish to see;
as we ate dinner, or watched TV it left droppings

between spoons and knives, would bite the corners
off bags of brown sugar and Basmati rice. We were

sleeping together again, but this time the central air
had gone, the mattress pulled onto the living room

floor beneath where a single window unit chugged.
We'd closed all the doors. It was early July. I was

still in the habit of being in love. The rain drummed
the sides of our duplex as you quoted your gospel,

that *a body wishes to be held, & held, & what can
you do about that?* I knew how to break a heart,

my own, already alone sitting on that mattress
like an island of cling, we clung to each other a little

longer than we should, to what we had left
—the mouse scurrying, all night, all along the edge.

Hunter Hazelton
Nocturne after Separation

I.

No one warned the pavement tonight.
　　　The radio mumbles a tune about God.
I have learned a man's mouth. Black air

opens its jaw, lets out its tongue—
　　　I am forgetting the brake. This vehicle
is not mine, but I am making it.

If God is omnipresent, why is he not here?

II.

The moon counts her deaths,
　　　pulls them out of the water. I am not one
　　　　　　　to be saved.
My grandmother reminds me to pray—
　　　　　　I pray *clutch* I pray *gear*—
I pray *insects on the windshield*
　　　　　　count miles per hour
& you do not answer.
Telephone poles like crosses absent of Christ,
　　　　　　tight wires at my throat.
Everything scares tonight—
　　　something's missing.

III.

I am at the cliff again, standing at its edge,
      the heels of my boot
            can feel death as capability—
                  convenient tragedy.
The audience, in their parked cars,
            watch a beast with his back to them.
They don't try to save him. They, too,
               want a show.
          They believe it means something
                            if he jumps.

IV.

I take the handgun & shoot the stars.
        Watch them fall into silent night.

Carnage victim to tires now.
        I look at the moon & say

                             Count.

V.

Pray count.
    Kill.
           Love.
God say wine.
    Pray drive.
          Drinking.   Losing.

Turn up the radio. Fill the silence.

VI.

Animals flayed, shocked like torn cords,
                    lay somewhere in the rain.

The road reserved for them. I hide
                    from light, hymns of distance—

sirens somewhere. If I am seen, there is certainty of place.
                    Touching man is a religion, but I've forgotten

how to love him.
                    What do you do when you lose your God?

I close my eyes, try to say his name, & pretend to remember
                    what his prayers felt like in my mouth.

VII.

Someone in the airport said, *Don't cry. He'll be back.*
          But to whom?
I cannot hide from the horror of this—
                    smiling people, water leaking
                              from the drinking fountain,
                    the sweater I have on,
          the way the moon, the coffee pot,
                                        potholes,
                    losing control,
                    I'm forgetting to drive.

Teach me how to pray. Teach me how to pray.

VIII.

My hands feel good wrapping around something
   other than themselves. To choke a thing to death. To play
   with omnipotence.
I am an outlaw, hauling through shadow, dodging
    streetlamp haloes—
   wrapped in the seraphim of a mechanical beast I've not tamed.
Panic of the engine.

On the highway, no one on either side,
   I drive, suicidal, closing my eyes, I try
     to cry a lullaby of—*Goodbye, baby, see you soon.*

I turn off the headlights.

L. A. Johnson
In Case of Emergency

Shallow cuts appear on my hands
                  as if made by invisible birds, their beaks
                      scratch warnings into my palms.
To quiet myself, I buy a tea kettle, a blanket,
                  a set of steel knives for cooking.

I dream I live in a landlocked lighthouse,
                  where a forest of ivy covers the wooden entrance.
                      My hair grows long. Not of any use
in my kingdom without coastline
                  or ship, my heart beats gold thin.

At two am, my body betrays me,
                  opens the door to witness
                      a lost dog, dirty figure in a coat
with no explanation, coming into the light
                  against a punctured rectangle of black.

He stands on the other side of the doorway, a gap
                  between floor tile and the frame. Neither
                      of us speaks. Heat rises from his face
like a veil, though he'll never be a bride,
                  before he pulls at my nightgown, lifts it

at first almost gentle as a cat's nuzzle.
                  I've hoped for this night
                      for I am governed by a fragile god
who keeps no time, who would tend
                  a fallow field forever. Each letter

he wrote fell across my bed like the fine dust
                of a season's first snow, a hush in the air
                      a rush held in the return address.
I never wrote back, transcribing instead the surface
                of a river, the surface of a mirror,

the words galloping in my head
                toward another life, what I would give up.
                      In the room with a view of the river,
I collected the letters like sharp objects,
        let them grow cold in the corner. Until

he stood unannounced in the night outside my house,
                no promise of anything, no explanation
                  of where he'd gone where time
stood still, every past forgotten
        like childhood. My body tried to hold

back my body, early brown blood
                staining the sheets we slept in.
                      All the while the knives waited
luminous and hidden in their drawer,
        glinting with excitement.

—Nominated by *Bennington Review*

Tracy Fuad
An Abridged History of Buttons

First, for ornamental purposes. A mud disk, spun
until it buzzed. Then, a method of adherence. This

to that, a coat closed tight against the wind. Bone,
shell, and vegetable ivory; knobs of knotted rope.

To be tight in the right places. To suggest their own
undoing. Some, containing tiny iron needles pointing

north to guide in war. Or punched from the mother
of pearl dragged up in Muscatine, stripped of meat

in chemical baths, workers paid by the blank until
the strike and town-wide riot. Before the ubiquitous

toggle, a simple switch. Then affixed to lettered slugs.
Then digits and a circuit. A keypad and cash register.

Pressing and depressing. Color coded to avoid
grave error. A badge against the war. Then mass

produced in plastic. Fifty-thousand migrant workers, slap-
bang in the middle of nowhere. A thing that can be

pressed toward irritation. Or with quotation marks
to emphasize the consequence. Or without effect

and only to suggest control at crosswalks and office
thermostats. One to drop the mustard gas, another

for the Tomahawks. To begin and end the sanctions.
To dial and to hang up. To eject the tape; to power

on, to press play, press record. And then, a flat
graphic. A coded event. A rectangle with a thin

shadow. To login, to reset, to send. To give consent.
Click to submit. Click to like. To enter

the site. To go back home. *Do you want to stay
on this page? Do you want to leave without finishing?*

Sometimes I don't want to know where north is.
I don't want to be a form so easily undone.

—Nominated by *Pacifica Literary Review*

Xiao Yue Shan
the coming of spring in the time of martial law

I could tell you this: marigolds are a night flower.
in the hour of my birth there were men in the streets,
some with knives and some between skin and some
peeling open buds with swollen hands trying to find
a home to hide in. my mother fingered a ripened
bowl of hot water, carving out upon its surface the lines
by which our family would occur. five tracks wavering
before being soothed to nothing. papa came in with
the hands of smoke around his mouth. a fingernail
pressed into the back of my neck. quiet now. children
rose like night-fires in those decades in which no one spoke
above a whisper, striking the petrified days with heads
black as matches. among the dead: old hua, teacher
jian, chien-sha from the building two doors down,
cheng-yi who said the food on the mainland was better,
aunt ren and her pockets full of small oranges, young
ko and her sweet daughter who had lost teeth the day
prior. each night we soothed time as if it were newborn,
as a song about marigolds bled through the radio
and we held death upon fingertips to count by. in those years
it was children like I that cut through our mothers spearing,
every life born is the possibility of one more loss.
worn patches in the cloth of the nation. salt of blood
in the mouth as familiar as anthem. *stay still, just like you're dead,*
was a game we played when we were young.

Lena Moses-Schmitt
Thrive

Today I find the neighbor's house transformed
      by a cloud of hydrangeas
crowded around his door—*an astonishment*
my friend once called them,
   the collective noun she designed for this dilation

of bright purple & blue. I'm jealous of these flowers, whose puberty & time
to thrive is so obvious you never have to wonder
as I do, heading into my thirtieth year,
if I must have missed something,
my own short window of shining.

I take photographs of the flowers on my phone.
It's the same impulse that makes me take photos of sunsets
though the image always develops deadened & small,
   the sun a wrinkled marigold head
      foggy in its wrap of cellophane.
Take being the crucial word, I'm stealing

      the sight & divorcing it
from environment, making the image portable,
aspirational because it's something I can hold—
      not quite celestial,

these hydrangeas, but each one still a sun
setting into the bush. I grow
so enamored, so astonished

(& then so enamored with my ability to still grow
      so astonished after thirty years spent on earth)

I almost bend to smell them
      —but then the neighbor comes out to the porch.
The wave of hydrangeas laps at his knees

& he looks at me like can I help you
& I force a laugh, say I was just taking pictures

of your beautiful flowers.
He smiles, holds out his palm,
      & says *That will be five dollars*

please & though it's a joke
it doesn't really feel like a joke
      it feels like maybe

he really does think the beauty
of the flowers in his front yard
is private not public

& maybe he's right
even though by now
the hydrangeas exist
      not just as an image on my phone
but in my mind, the way I must exist

somewhere in the mind of the man
who earlier at the bus stop plucked me with his eyes
      going up & down
           & crooned   *You made my eyesight*
a whole lot better this morning

and later I'll post my photos of these hydrangeas
to the feed
my personal memory of them

now communal, each bloom a symbol
deceptively public

as a woman
on the street

each picture
insisting   *I'm happy I'm happy*

&

    I'm here,
bright

& last ditch
    as a signal flare

Max McDonough
Incunabula Just Before

The courthouse garden, during the last
rounds of my mother's trial, pleasant
side yard to justice, was throbbing

with pollen, each split-open flower
a slow-motion sneeze
as my brother wiped his hand,

snotty, across the bench's arm, licked
what remained, and slicked the spit
on his too-large dress pants. I didn't

know the names—black-eyed Susan,
maybe hyacinth—but I knew the colors
obscured a pattern underneath

only insects could see, their eyes
compounding frequencies
I couldn't fathom, as the midday sun

struck the garden a near shadowless
glow, and bees droned from petal
to petal. I sat on the bench,

trying to guess the designs hidden
from me, until it was half
past, and I was summoned

back to the courtroom, my turn,
to testify against her.

John Patrick McShea

After Wading Through the Marsh of Gilgo Beach for Nineteen Months, the Good Old Boys Eventually Uncover the Skeletal Remains of Shannan Gilbert Tucked in a Very Tough, Desolate, Tangled Mess, as Well as the Bodies of Other Women

        Help us understand.

Across the shore bodies of women are found dismembered in burlap
do you all need a reason why?

Isn't it strange, how a body exits to bone?

There are things that grow even after death

Through what do we wade?

Salt grass
chokecherry and some beach plum silvery sea-myrtle
      lines of anglers and the migration of striped bass
transitory rainstorm a shrinking shoreline   fissures of erosion
        a fleet of vessels beneath the horizon

Have these women been killed because they were whores?

They clutched life from any palm that offered

What emits this light?

Pleiades the seven sisters and the daughters of Pleione
have fallen to sea   and were carried by the tide
      now they rise on the beach as rain craters the sand

What powers do women hold?

On the shore my lover imbued a stone with her first menstrual blood
she kept it bedside before it vanished

Explain this to us.

Seduction is rooted in divinity
and the rosette-shelled crab is stolen by both shrew and tern
from whom do you steal the most?

Should we take Shannan's remains elsewhere?

Her body is inert and has been here for months
to move a still thing is unnatural

What will happen to Shannan's mother?

She will be stabbed two hundred and twenty-seven times
and beaten with a fire extinguisher by her other daughter

Is this the catasterism of Shannan Maria Gilbert?

Of whom Zeus made stars he first made doves
consequence of Orion's obsessions
even lost Merope stalked by the hunter
Shannan ascends the sky

The rain has stopped.

A storm as transient as all things
in how many ways are you vagrants?

Is there room for a whippoorwill?

If you want a whippoorwill then I give you a whippoorwill   lucent and alone
this nightjar now guards the marsh

Kristina Faust
Diorama

We went out the back door into thick fog and drove to school.
Each tree was a portrait of a tree, every dog a soloist.
All sounds traveled only as far as breath.

It's like a diorama, I said, pretending to win the game. *Have a good day.*
You stepped out into it and I steered toward home, resolving to find
a shoe box, paper, and bristled trees.

In the layered world only the nearest things were certain.
The next nearest were as they could be if softly presented behind waxed paper.
Anything else was lost to speculation.

The legs of the water tower might rise forty stories. The corn field could go on for miles.
The door to the school might open into a cloud, and when you walked through it,
you fell and fell.

So the satisfaction of the diorama is in the arrest of the loved thing.
A deer, perhaps, in manageable miniature bowing her head to cedar-stained water
but never drinking, and never shot.

Later, if you sit with me, I'll paint hills like eyelids,
eyelids beyond eyelids, fading to the sky.

—Nominated by *minnesota review*

Tanya Grae
The Line of a Girl

1

At sunrise, our caryatid
stands at the kitchen window
& white embroidered curtains
diffuse daylight into her glow.

I study her silhouette:
the load-bearer, the muse,
my grandmother as Atlas, yet
Smyrna moves outside this

woman—within her history
another South, different endings
my child mind can't perceive.
She is a belle smoldering

with cigarette. Her drawn lines
surrendered, illuminate
& sear. Scythe. Burning. Joyce,
the lighthouse of hours, the late.

2

In the afternoons, I draw close
& practice reading books aloud.
She listens for a lilt, even in prose,
signifying import with her brow,

generations of correction
so I will speak well, genteel,
the diction of illusion.
My savored prize, her smile,

exhales the gray as she grinds
a filter into her wedding silver
ashtray; white flags on gristled
embers bear her wreck, red stain.

3

She fills her glass & it empties
& again. Days I watch until
my mouth is dry. I am off to play;
she is lost in sight, the undertow

of entertaining oneself when lonely
& not alone—all the comfort is outside.
I spend hours underneath the mimosa,
the fern lace light of its shade, jazz-

handed pink in constellation.
From wherever, I am her Black-eyed
Susan here. Wide acres over it all, free.
A girl running. *Jesus, can you see me?*

I feel so small—not as little
as a thrush or the ruby-throats
tongue deep in the honeysuckle
with furious wings, not easy to be.

But she was that sudden goddess
amid small town bourgeoisie,
out of air. An invisible net—
is it so intangible, the life

versus living? This, her way out:
arranged, comfortable years
with a gentle man, without want.
What of a settled home, why fear?

4

Dear heart—the same words
of my mother, the appearance
of elevation, the right tone,
the pleasing smile. Beauty cries

over a bitten lip, nails dug deep
into a fisted palm. Years later, this
same bed I've made, this lie I keep,
summons her presence, uncalm.

Does my tremor wrench the line—
that silver cord, that river
of provenance between us?
I feel her in the curtain weight,

the sail, the ballast. My house reels
adrift as the floors settle & moan,
the walls, my head spinning. *Jesus*—
do you feel it too?

Jennifer Manthey
Puer Malus

He is running and it's not allowed.
        An indoor playground attendant
        watched him til he ran,
til she could squeeze his arm,
fingers leaving brief marks that burn
like misplaced stars,
constellation we could draw on the night sky
of his skin and name
Puer Malus. Her moon face
shines with its borrowed light
and she points to the sign with the rules,
other children running by
in their wild bedhead,
my son's lines crisp, pick in my purse
to keep it neat.
To love a Black boy. To break
daily and learn
what you should have already known:
I drove with a broken tail-light
for a couple years in college,
to my boyfriend's apartment on Larpenteur Ave.,
same street Philando was shot
for his not-broken taillight.
        Turn a country over
        and see how it's made.
When I was young I was a perfectionist,
spent high school and college
with straight A's and my fingers

down my throat. It's crushing—
how he will need
to be even more perfect.

—Nominated by *Radar Poetry*

Cara Dees

After Arriving Home from Church and Learning Our Dogs Were Shot, Their Bodies in the Fields

For weeks I walked the shoulderless road,
calling.   *Welcome,*
the wind psalmed back, *your feed*

is wanting teeth. The swamp
sighed odes   to silence, concerned
with its bounty of skunk,

its possum. I called to my mild
black dog with   delicate eyes,
to my timid golden dog missing

a leg, to the modest calm
of our house,   driven out
entire, to the hollow silage.

I walked and called. I thought,
voices get tired, too,   they run away
with the body, and the body

mislays so easily its claw and howl.
Like how,   twenty years later,   I watch
you—your blunt silence

among the summering of the hymnals,
driven out   of yourself
on the velvet interior, calling me.

—Nominated by *Crazyhorse*

Kevin Phan
Punchline

I.

Among artists frozen into snowbanks,
among riot shields & drone strikes, no. 3
main ballast tanks, *hands up, don't shoot,*
blue moon hydrangea, tearjerkers & riffraff,
a whale of a car crash, Aleppo in ruins,
another new crime spree, sidewalk vomit,
pizza chef migraines, the feathers that feed
us, kindness forgiving one day for the next,
let's dance in river before we go home,
then wait.

II.

Wait—for ghosts to be rinsed clean in
the light, for the Discovery Channel to
reveal, for savior figures big as bouncers, for
forensics to be shipped back from the lab,
for shotgun fire to dissolve into flowers mid-
flight. Another colored body growing colder.
One headline [adds to / complicates / hides
/ reveals / replaces] another, grief translated
into anger, something always on fire, vacant
fire extinguisher, beneath bridges, in libraries,
under stairwells, frost burnt transients slip in
needles. Say yes.

III.

Yes. Hours, brighten into months, knives saw clean through flesh, let fish swim through hoops of light, cocaine energize our spectrums, bright rabbit blood race to the moon, let the aspens shiver their *fuckyes*, let the river answer, first & foremost, let her answer. An ear of listening to the earth—can you hear them? Listen on.

IV.

Can you hear them? They're saying: *they snapshot my terror before emptying their guns*, saying *I reached out completely to every hurting heart & my heart also hurt*, saying *we cut ourselves on sharp & rough*, they say *sweet sticky asphalt, I'm down on my knees waiting for the Lord to come—please come*, saying *traded in two dollars for a nasty can of Coke*.

V.

Can you hear them? They shake like a quarry giving in—reach for a handle where a fake doorknob was painted on, self-report missing in the bathroom mirror. Earth-stuck, dreaming up the cherrymilk of heaven. & Now I know what I want: I want to remodel the absences in my life, summer skin all winter, enforcement officers outfitted w/ corrective lenses, less of this hospital in the crying light. Magical thinking to truncate terror, "our children are angels in God's heaven," *olly olly oxen free* meaning Treyvon, Jordan Davis, Renisha McBride, Eric Garner, Michael Brown, LaQuan McDonald, Tamir Rice, Baltimore, Detroit, East St. Louis, Appalachia, East Timor, *come out, come out,* (oh, how we fucking wish to remake your home.)

VI.

Imagine home, a somewhere for every someone, praise for the riff-raff, February forgiveness parades, transitions between genders, enough soul-fire to clear off a layer of dead skin. It's how we *really* make America great again. Even the man walking down the street blasted on discount vodka longs to be home. Listen, he's singing (this time) of apples & blankets, moonshine & hickeys—(this deadbeat eyesore)—& soon he too will drop to one knee & collapse in human laughter.

—Nominated by *Cincinnati Review*

Rachel Morgenstern-Clarren
Quintland

Yvonne, Annette, Cécile, Émilie & Marie Dionne—the first quintuplets known to survive infancy—lived at Quintland, a Canadian tourist attraction, from 1934 to 1943.

I.

Women in matching dresses zip us into matching dresses. They weave ribbon through our whorled locks when we wake & brush them into five crooked streams before bed. We roll on the ground just to knock the bobby pins out of place, just to feel their hands again in our hair.

II.

Yellow tape cinches our skin; they speak to each other in our numbers. The nursery's filled with colors but we can only touch our own. If we cry or shout, pens move quickly behind their clipboards. Ink to paper like teeth against teeth.

III.

The man in white puts metal to our hearts. His small light floods our ears & eyes. He strikes both knees with a rubber triangle, smiling each time we kick.

IV.

Through whispers, we pump our legs across the lawn, singing. All we can see is the screen around us, not the people gathered behind. Never their faces, just shadows, growing long.

V.

They say many fingers bathed us in olive oil when we were born. An open stove lit the embers of our limbs. Each time our lungs barked like stray dogs for scraps, an eyedropper fed us cow's milk, boiled water, syrup, rum.

VI.

When we dance around our bedroom, sisters circling sisters, I see myself repeating in an angled mirror. The kind I imagine a mother keeps on her vanity. That she'd look into as she wiped the red from her smile, spotting me, alone, at the door.

Augusta Funk
Guidebook

I wake the Christmas duck at midnight.
Snap back the neck, tie the feet together and let hang
an unborn child come from outside of me, dreaming
of the days I choked over an egg and slice of bread.

How my heart rattled, hollow as a fist,
rotted meat no feast could fatten
in a checkered gown licking honey from the lips of warm foil.
How when I hid under a chair, my spine softened.

Beneath my eyelids, Grandmother hovers with her cold
peppermint tea. The bird
waits: I muss the feathers with oil and pluck them,
one by one, from rubber skin, push down the blade
to crack the breastplate, and fold back the meat.

The white pearly nectar of my heart glistens in my chest.
Grandmother says *eat*.

—Nominated by *Memorious*

J.P. Grasser
Lesson in Winter

The Sandhills were fixed in ice.
The buckwheat chaffs looked breakable,

like the fletching of a glass arrow
or a mouse's contorted skeleton, housed

within an owl pellet. The night before,
we caught a possum in a plastic bucket

under the house's cement foundation.
The foundation was cracked from years of scale

and thaw. Aunt Carol handed me your .22,
so I put a bullet behind its ear, then cleaned

the gun. I used solvent and a swatch of linen,
just how you showed me that summer.

Because the world was so bright,
we were late to your funeral. We kept running

off the road. When the possum thawed
and mealworms ate their way out, I looked

through the window they'd opened
in its gut and a litter looked placidly back.

Kelly Grace Thomas
Small Things

The webs of Walnut Creek are all spun
white. In our new town, I notice each
grocery store glare. Sticky stares
follow Omid down each aisle.

Still my love keeps quiet
hands. Wears kindness like salt
and pepper stubble. I study him
as he hums to houseplants.

It's been hard for me to learn a love
so gentle. To believe him when he chants
me close. Hushes *gorgeous* until I fall

asleep. In the morning, he scrambles eggs.
Spatula in hand, he spots the lonely
daddy-longlegs in a quiet corner. The wall weaver
nestled next to light. He says, *needing a home
is such a small thing to be forgiven for.*

He lets the delicate geometry
stay. I am slow to learn
how to handle a living thing. I study Omid

as he smiles at spiders. I ask him
how? His speech soft as saffron, breath, a net
I lean against. He tells me he's been called a terrorist
more times than he can count. His answer: save something

smaller. Call each a guest. Leave all doors open.
*Just because the world has called something
poison,* he says, *doesn't mean we kill it.*

Cate Lycurgus
Screenshot

Logging in hours katydid-folded
                    up at my desk in the glitched light
        of a rain-laid weekday, my frame
flickers: half-me half-
                stick insect
                        virtually fixed
    to the furniture;
                    by virtue it holds
that like a virus—one does not exist. With home

        page a place-
holder, I start every day with a search. Also
            on my list of to-dos: free up
        some memory, & await no word. No
blue circle marked un-
                        read, received but plangent
            & left to glowing
as ghost-
        text on the night-
            stand nightly as clocks turn over—
        & I do
            refresh, wake, pour
clouded whey
        off the top of a yogurt carton, save
                    the rest
for tomorrow;
the same, it will water
                    & every strain: a strengthening

By *strengthening* I mean *increase* mean *unceasing*
     rainbow spiral growing to bystanding
panic—nothing
        to do but re-
            load the choose-your-own
     desperate story: over-
          drawn, over-committed, dosed or sentenced
or just shot
         all over the news. Old, how we crash
        in the same
        no-fanfare with the laptop's fan

taking off, & what did I think
              a flutter of clicks
         might assuage, what
       balm my surfing make—

    in attempts to web world-
wide, I backlit the bowl of now-strained yogurt

its Red-4 Blue-2 berry-blend, plus granola more
       deadly than cookies; I posed with some leg
          in another post; logged my miles

borough to coast; wrote what I wrote I was
       thrilled to have written—

   so say it, be done with the saying of it:

that breakfast spread was on sale at Kroger,
            but I show it off

     for you. Have little virtue &

know the tattoos
under all my dearests' clothes, growing up

through skin. Mostly I take
the same town loop past the high school, its stand of redwoods,
same old system
of trees.

Am trying to re-vise Wednesday.

Pitch a right-
angled
lap at every café; still haven't mastered
copy-pasting a meadows' mist; a dance hall's

insistent throb & simply
scroll past
a flag of sunsets somehow flung
across the sky

day after day after day—
if they do not save
what will?

Since each cloud
holds the backdrop
that we most
need to see, or imagine
ours to be &

if no one else
 need be present
  for the pixels' darkening out—
 let *was,* once,
   code

  for *enough*

Kassidi Jones

A Conversation with My Therapist / A Letter I Want to Send to My Ex-Boyfriend (But Will Keep for Myself)

You know you can stop eating when you're full
instead of finishing a plate you no longer want

of all the things we've learned from each other,
pare it down to the porcelain.

I know you feel the need to purge
the things that sustain you,

other people's guilt, other people's shame—
the things that give you purpose

but consider this: even your open mouth
has multiple functions. Call out

cannot hold a prayer for every sinner. Faith
in the name of a love we both outgrew

if you need to be found, if you're hurting
Swallow water, swallow honestly. Do not

(please be honest with yourself)
split me into both a mother and a child.

take another pulchrum worm into your mouth
and blame your appetite for the hunger

You are addicted to the way burden makes you fever,
because you're the only one you have the power to punish.

What I'm trying to say is
are you sure that you want to be well?:

there are more things to do with a lesson than suffer, so
stop forging a martyr out of your own name,

if so
be well

You are still good
without crucifixion.

Devon Walker-Figueroa
Private Lessons

The third thing I learned was to surround
        myself with shapely
space. My teacher bound

my toes in turquoise tape—type an ovine
        foot requires when trouble nests
within. I'd bow at close of class, as if I weren't

        the only one allowed
inside the room. He went by "Cloud"
        & had designs on dying

soon. Each week, another noun
        gone missing from his mouth. I
mean, a tooth defined

        by a "toxic" crown.
I think I thought that he divined the ground
        when he said, "don't

look at the floor: it's just a sign
        you don't trust me
to tell you if it disappears." He wound around

his throat each day camphoric
        scarves & I resigned what all I could
to expert touch & expiration. He would crouch

at my blistered feet, a sweat-
        stained supplicant bent
on aligning my stubborn frame with his

        dream, bent on forming a farmer's
daughter into a true
        danseuse. What use

in maligning his methods now? His name
        is just a sound
I hear in sleep. "Hate

the sin, but not
        the sinner," said a God-
fearer at his service, as to astound, as to revive

rumors of unkempt relations. Our inner-
        most contours grew a little
too perceptible but pleasing

to our eyes. Sure, we'd found
        a reciprocity: he knew
the bread winner in my family couldn't win

much, so he'd taken me
        on for a song—no faltering
in it. He'd set me spinning

        round him while he clapped. Call it keeping
time. Call it manáge. Reader,
        we worked with our wrong

deadline, too full
      of ourselves & an ability to make
an artful thing. I was twelve. He held

      my spine at start
of class & gave a practiced
      jerk, mock broke my neck in the name

of a pleasing line. Him, swallowed up
      in a red robe. Me, supine in nude leotard. "Stop
moving," he said, but his palsies unwound

in my heel & bowed arch. He's managed to stay
      as ache. In the wood box, cinder.
The first thing I learned was to hold my tongue.

Justin Jannise

"Until then, I'm stuck with the person that I am."

—*a friend*

I'm stuck with your teeth, including
the one you chipped on a fork
at the Olive Garden, surrounded by
cheerleaders, and the molar that's
still sensitive to cold after an $800 root canal
paid out of pocket.
I'm stuck with your lack of wisdom,
with your clammy hands
and allergy to penicillin.
I'm attached to your addictions.
I crave what you crave and must undertake
the task of denying it to you, at times,
for our mutual benefit.
I have no discipline when it comes
to loving your family. Even if we broke up,
I would still be friends with them.
They're so wildly talkative I can see why
you believed them when they said
you were adopted.
I'm glued to your long showers
and emergency travel plans, your tendency
to disappear without warning or explanation.
You are careless with goodbyes:
either blurting or dragging them out.
I'm married to your belly fat and hairy ass.
I own a share
of your ability to know things first.
Women who are secretly pregnant,

men hiding their affairs.
I am tied to your impatience with small talk,
your road rage, your ugly tattoos.
I am in quicksand with your death wish
as well as your knack for self-preservation.
I am pinned, like a butterfly collection,
to the blue velvet of your stubbornness.
I am as dear to you as a button
but baffled by how infrequently
you tell me this. I am crazy about
your inner gorilla, your outer flamingo.
Every day you find some new way
to smite me. The Venus flytrap does not know
it eats flies, which leads me to wonder
how much the fly knows about its manner
of death. How large does a brain have to be
to be capable of denial?
Mornings I lie awake for hours
before I can move. I've automated
the clock to brief me on the latest
travesties, preferring global discord
to the doves' nonstop coos, as I wrestle
with what makes me this way
cocooned in living too close to work.
Today it took listening to the same report
at 5, 6, 7, and 8 before I could rise
like Dracula in his nightgown
and hustle through my preparations.
I've been tempted to call the station.
More variety, please.

Skyler Osborne
The Magician's World

Perfect loop of the spirit
eating itself like a haunted ice cream cone—
once my grandmother opened her parasol
at the dinner table, her mind fallen out
to name her stray children. Poverty
no longer monstrous appeared
like a black tooth in bathwater.
I summoned myself to the backyard,
lobbed sharpened branches at the sky
and closed my eyes. No wonders
in that town. The train splintered the trees.
The local saints stapled roses to the barn.

A man can divide a sycamore and still love God.
A man can decapitate himself and still live
in the magician's world. Moss in my hair,
I sold old clothes and a rabbit skeleton
to the thrift center. I followed the purple blade
of light slung over the Labrador's ear,
I loved everything she loved forever.
The analog voices of the dead flared
from the radio the first time
digging a hole in the forest where I buried
a mannequin with the chest excised
and replaced by a bag of small money.
I waited for crime, somewhere
a criminal leaving hell to find it there

beneath the X and last with slow anatomy
like all the people standing in their driveways,
smoke rolling through their teeth. What a refuge.

Alan Pelaez Lopez
The Spine of Gorée Island: (contrapuntal)

I made my first rag doll at three	Our healer reminds us she's not eternal
It's a coming-of-age of sorts	Each child must tend to *their* body
Where we learn to identify pain	(No one ever expected this amount of pain)
In our bodies	There are stories
At the Maison des Esclaves	My body remembers these stories
I am three again / Learning	Of dispossession
And unlearning things about	Those who took us
Pain	And the water
The cell downstairs looks	Awful
Like the child detention center	There is no way out
My dear friend recalls	The intimacy of this haunting
Twenty years after her escape/	Reminds me of my crossing
The walls remind me of abuela's	Quiet sounds of leaving
Home/ And these walls	One must face
They are screaming / At the Maison	—Masters lived here and
des Esclaves, I am three again	There is French, Spanish and Dutch
There is pain in my small intestine	And here, we are reminded that
Though it could've been stopped	We just weren't people

Liam Powell
Ellipses of the South

If a forest admires you with calm grey eyes,
every car rolls slowly by.
                           If there are stages here
and on them stand blue marines,
I came up with my lover.
Navies can be raised, but not without citrus.
Then the Navy men hoard oranges.
Then they sway
about the entrance to the gala
                                 like fireflies
in sawgrass, like drunks in a ritual invisible
to the moneyed.
                        If every car rolls slowly by
it wasn't the large fire that razed us,
but the hundred embers
that burned into our sleep.
Then we walked into the forest twice:
                           once to find an orchard
and again to find an orchard,
but could go no deeper than the fringe.
This was one of many gaps in the landscape.
If all of the action happens offscreen,
the cowboy
                    has been riding in the wrong direction.
Then I came here with a strange partner,
made stranger by the southern light.
If there is a voice speaking in parallel
to the movement of the clouds,
                             it would not be laughing.

Emily Luan
Aubade in Milk White

My father used to be a manager at a beverage factory. At the end of the day when everyone else had left, he'd fill one of the vats with leftover milk and steam it until it was hot. Then, he'd leave his clothes on the factory floor and take a long milk bath.

Every so often I remember this story and I won't know if I've dreamt it—my father in the milk fog and silver machinery. Those were the days my father ran up debts of beer and cigarettes at the local store and before my long-haired mother began working at the factory. I imagine his body disappearing into white, his full head of black hair the first exclamation of a calligrapher's brush on rice paper. Did he long for a woman who could become my mother? Did small sounds in the silence frighten him? I want to inherit loneliness from the scene but what do I know of my father's dreams? I'm still creating my own mythology of moving water, the field mice tunneling through ice in deep winter. When I draw a bath, I'm usually trying to take myself from sadness and into sleep. And in the blackest hour of morning my head calls back my body, like the bird that circles high above, singing 回，回，回。

Acknowledgments

Kemi Alabi's "Soft & Beautiful Just For Me Relaxer, No-Lye Conditioning Creme, Children's Regular" previously appeared in *BOAAT*.

Megan J. Arlett's "Jaw" previously appeared in *Passages North*.

Meriwether Clarke's "Follow the Leader" previously appeared in *Gigantic Sequins*.

Cara Dees's "After Arriving Home from Church and Learning Our Dogs Were Shot, Their Bodies in the Fields" previously appeared in *Crazyhorse*.

Gen Del Raye's "Litmus Test" previously appeared in *Up North Lit*.

Katherine Fallon's "Letters from the Farm" previously appeared in *Colorado Review*.

Kristina Faust's "Diorama" previously appeared in *minnesota review*.

M.K. Foster's "Aubade with Dolly Parton on Vinyl" previously appeared in *The Account*.

Tracy Fuad's "An Abridged History of Buttons" previously appeared in *Pacifica Literary Review*.

Augusta Funk's "Guidebook" previously appeared in *Memorious*.

Robin Gow's "rice & rain " previously appeared in *Poetry*.

Tanya Grae's "The Line of a Girl" previously appeared in *Bayou*.

J.P. Grasser's "Lesson in Winter" previously appeared in *The Sewanee Review*.

Mitchell Jacobs's "Chronicle with a Series of Vessels" previously appeared in *Passages North*.

L. A. Johnson's "In Case of Emergency" previously appeared in *Bennington Review*.

Keith Kopka's "For a Moment I Feel Immortal, or, Rather, Disappointed" previously appeared in *Passages North*.

Jennifer Manthey's "Puer Malus" previously appeared in *Radar Poetry*.

Maya Marshall's "[midnight with a new moon]" previously appeared in *Muzzle Magazine*.

John Patrick McShea's "After Wading Through the Marsh..." previously appeared in *Ninth Letter*.

Skyler Osborne's "The Magician's World" previously appeared in *No Tokens*.

Charlie Peck's "Noise" previously appeared in *Quarterly West*.

Kevin Phan's "Punch Line" previously appeared in *Cincinnati Review*.

Ösel Jessica Plante's "Poem with Duplex, Mouse, & Line by Larry Levis" previously appeared in *Stirring Lit*.

Liam Powell's "Ellipses of the South" previously appeared in *Gasher*.

Joy Priest's "American Honey" previously appeared in *Southern Cultures*.

Molly Bess Rector's "Self-Portrait as Nuclear Fallout " previously
appeared in *The Collagist*.

Shannon Sankey's "Lonesome Errand" previously appeared in
minnesota review.

Kelly Grace Thomas's "Small Things " previously appeared in
Rise Up Review.

Jihyun Yun's "Menstruation Triptych" previously appeared in
Blue Mesa Review.

Contributors' Notes

KEMI ALABI is the author of *The Lion Tamer's Daughter* (YesYes Books, 2020) with poems and essays in *The Rumpus, Guernica, Catapult, The Boston Review*, and elsewhere. They lead Echoing Ida, a Forward Together community of Black women and nonbinary writers, and live in Chicago.

MEGAN J. ARLETT was born in the United Kingdom, grew up in Spain, and now lives in Texas where she is pursuing her PhD. She is an editor at the Plath Poetry Project. The recipient of two Academy of American Poets Prizes, her work has appeared or is forthcoming in *Best New British and Irish Poets, The Kenyon Review, Ninth Letter, Passages North, Third Coast*, and elsewhere.

MARY LENOIR BOND is a writer, editor, and herbalist. She graduated from University of Southern California with a BA in English/creative writing and holds an MFA from Pacific University in writing/poetry. She has published online journalistic pieces about silent films and fairy tales, and serves as a fiction editor for *The Molotov Cocktail* and a poetry editor for *Phantom Drift*. Mary has work published in *Prairie Schooner, december*, The Johns Hopkins University Project MUSE site, *Rust + Moth*, and more. She currently resides in Portland, Oregon, where she immerses herself in organic gardening and aromatherapy.

MARGARET CIPRIANO's visual and written work has appeared or is forthcoming in *Quarterly West, McSweeney's, DIAGRAM, West Branch, Ninth Letter, Mid-American, Copper Nickel, Poetry Northwest*, and others. She was recently a finalist for Greg Grummer Poetry Award and the former managing editor of *The Journal*. She lives in Seattle, Washington.

MERIWETHER CLARKE is a poet and educator living in Los Angeles. She holds degrees in poetry from Northwestern University and UC Irvine. Her work has recently been seen in *Prairie Schooner, Tin House, Gigantic Sequins, The Superstition Review*, and elsewhere. She is the author of the chapbook *Twenty-First Century Woman* (Dancing Girl, 2019).

RACHAEL UWADA CLIFFORD is a writer and poet living in Baltimore. The daughter of Nigerian immigrants, she was born in Tennessee and grew up in Georgia and New Mexico. She received her MFA from the Writing Seminars at Johns Hopkins University, where she also taught creative writing. She has received fellowships from the Cave Canem Foundation, Kimbilio, The Mastheads, Ox-Bow, and the Maryland State Arts Council. She won first place in *Glimmer Train*'s Short Story Award for New Writers contest and her work appears in the fall 2019 issue.

JAMES DAVIS's poems have appeared or are forthcoming in *32 Poems, Copper Nickel, The Gay & Lesbian Review, Harpur Palate, Hobart*, and elsewhere; his stories have appeared in *American Short Fiction* and *NANO Fiction*. He is a 2019 Mastheads resident and a graduate of the University of Florida MFA Program. He lives in Denver.

NOAH DAVIS grew up in Tipton, Pennsylvania, and writes about the Allegheny Front. Davis's manuscript *Of This River* was selected by George Ella Lyon for the 2019 Wheelbarrow Emerging Poet Book Contest from Michigan State University's Center for Poetry, and his poems and prose have appeared in *Orion, North American Review, River Teeth, Sou'wester*, and *Chautauqua* among others. His work has been nominated for the Pushcart Prize by *Poet Lore* and *Natural Bridge*, and he has been awarded a Katharine Bakeless Nason Fellowship at the Bread Loaf Writer's Conference and the 2018 Jean Ritchie Appalachian Literature Fellowship from Lincoln Memorial University. Davis is a third-year MFA candidate at Indiana University.

CARA DEES is the author of the debut collection, *Exorcism Lessons in the Heartland*, selected by Ada Limón for the 2018 Barrow Street Book Prize. Currently a PhD candidate at the University of Cincinnati, her work appears or is forthcoming in *Best New Poets 2016*, *Crazyhorse*, *Gulf Coast*, *Harvard Review*, *Poetry Daily*, *The Southeast Review*, and elsewhere.

GEN DEL RAYE is half Japanese and was born and raised in Kyoto, Japan. Currently, he lives in Minneapolis, Minnesota. He is the winner of the Up North Poetry Prize and the Great Midwest Poetry Contest, both in 2019.

LUC DIGGLE's work has appeared in *The Café Review* and *The Columbia Review*. He lives in rural Vermont and is a graduate of the Bennington Writing Seminars.

PATRICK JAMES ERRINGTON is the author of two chapbooks, *Glean* (ignitionpress, 2018) and *Field Studies* (Clutag Press, 2019), and the French translator of PJ Harvey's poetry collection *Au creux de la main* (Éditions l'Âge d'Homme, 2017). Born in Canada, he currently lives in Scotland where he teaches at the University of Edinburgh.

KATHERINE FALLON's poems have appeared in *Meridian*, *Empty Mirror*, *Permafrost*, *Juked*, *Foundry*, *Rust + Moth*, and others. Her chapbook, *The Toothmakers' Daughters*, is available through Finishing Line Press. She assists in editing *Terrible Orange Review*, teaches in the Department of Writing and Linguistics at Georgia Southern University, and shares domestic square footage with two cats and her favorite human, who helps her zip her dresses.

KRISTINA FAUST lives and works in Grand Rapids, Michigan. Her poems have appeared recently in *Washington Square Review*, *Harvard Review*, *The Common*, *The Georgia Review*, and elsewhere. She received the 2018 Disquiet Literary Prize for poetry.

M.K. FOSTER is a poet and Renaissance literature scholar from Birmingham, Alabama. Her poetry has appeared or is forthcoming in *Boston Review, The Gettysburg Review, Crazyhorse, The Columbia Review, Gulf Coast, The Account, Rattle, The Journal, Sixth Finch, B O D Y*, and elsewhere. Her poetry has been recognized with a Gulf Coast Poetry Prize, an Academy of American Poets Prize, and Pushcart Prize nominations, among other honors. Foster is currently completing her PhD in the Hudson Strode Program in Renaissance Studies at the University of Alabama, where her interests include nature, monstrosity, horror, mass extinction, sharks, and Dolly Parton. For additional notes and links, please visit marykatherinefoster.com.

TRACY FUAD is a poet from Minnesota and a graduate of the Rutgers–Newark MFA in Creative Writing Program. Her work has appeared in *Poetry, Washington Square Review, Bennington Review*, and the *Boston Review*'s anthology *What Nature*. She is the author of the chapbook *Imagined State* and the art book *DAD DAD DAD DAD DAD DAD DAD* (TxtBooks, 2019). She lives and works in Kurdistan.

AUGUSTA FUNK is a queer poet from the Midwest. She has been published in *The Massachusetts Review, Passages North*, and *Tinderbox*, among others. Currently, she lives in Ann Arbor, Michigan, where she is a Zell Fellow at the University of Michigan.

ROBIN GOW is a queer and trans poet editor and educator based in New York City.

TANYA GRAE is the author of *Undoll* (YesYes Books, 2019). Her poems and essays have appeared in *The American Poetry Review, Ploughshares, AGNI, Prairie Schooner, Post Road*, and other journals. She is currently a Kingsbury Fellow at Florida State University where she is finishing her PhD in creative writing.

A former Wallace Stegner Fellow, J.P. GRASSER is a PhD candidate at the University of Utah, where he edits *Quarterly West*.

HUNTER HAZELTON is a poet and educator from Phoenix, Arizona. His work has been published by Scribendi and Storm of Blue Press.

PARKER HOBSON is a poet from Louisville, Kentucky, whose poems have appeared or are forthcoming in *Conduit* and *The Santa Ana River Review*. In 2018, he received an MFA in creative writing from the University of Kentucky, and he was recently the recipient of an Emerging Artist Award from the Kentucky Arts Council. He is also a radio producer and a songwriter.

MITCHELL JACOBS lives in Vientiane, Laos, and teaches English at the National University of Laos. His poems appear in journals such as *Gulf Coast*, *Ninth Letter*, *Passages North*, *Ploughshares*, and *Poetry Northwest*.

JUSTIN JANNISE studied poetry at Yale and the Iowa Writers' Workshop and is currently a PhD student at the University of Houston. His work has appeared or is forthcoming in *Copper Nickel*, *New Ohio Review*, *Yale Review*, and *Zócalo Public Square*. He is the editor-in-chief of *Gulf Coast* and the recipient of an Inprint Marion Barthelme Prize.

L. A. JOHNSON is from California. She is the author of the chapbook *Little Climates* (Bull City Press, 2017). She is currently pursuing her PhD in literature and creative writing from the University of Southern California, where she is a Provost's Fellow. Her poems have recently appeared or are forthcoming in *The American Poetry Review*, *Blackbird*, *Prairie Schooner*, *The Southern Review*, *TriQuarterly*, and other journals. Find her online at la-johnson.com.

KASSIDI JONES a poet cautiously representing Connecticut. She is pursuing her PhD in English and African American Studies at Yale.

A 2017 *Callaloo* fellow and a self-proclaimed Scrabble master, Kassidi is an alumna of the Excelano Project, UPenn's premier spoken word poetry group. Her work can be found in *Backbone Press, Winter Tangerine,* and *Crab Fat Magazine.*

KEITH KOPKA is the author of *Count Four* (University of Tampa Press, 2020). His poetry and criticism have recently appeared in *The International Journal of the Book, Mid-American Review, New Ohio Review, Berfrois, Ninth Letter,* and many others. Kopka is the recipient of the 2017 International Award for Excellence from the Books, Publishing & Libraries Research Network. He is also a senior editor at *Narrative,* as well as the co-founder and the director of operations for Writers Resist.

EMILY LUAN is a Taiwanese American poet. A recipient of fellowships from Bread Loaf Writers' Conference, the Community of Writers at Squaw Valley, Art Farm, and the Fine Arts Work Center, her poetry has been published or is forthcoming in *Washington Square Review, The Offing, The Margins, PANK, Grist,* and elsewhere. She holds an MFA in poetry from Rutgers University–Newark.

CATE LYCURGUS's poetry has appeared or is forthcoming in *The American Poetry Review, Tin House, Orion,* and elsewhere. A 2014 Ruth Lilly Fellowship finalist, she has also received scholarships from Bread Loaf and Sewanee Writers' Conferences and was named one of *Narrative*'s 30 Under 30 Featured Writers. Cate lives south of San Francisco, California, where she conducts interviews for *32 Poems* and teaches professional writing.

JENNIFER MANTHEY earned her MFA from Hamline University in Saint Paul, Minnesota. She is a reader for *Palette Poetry* and teaches classes at The Loft. Her work can be found in journals such as *Prairie Schooner, Calyx, Crab Orchard Review, RHINO,* and *Tinderbox Poetry Journal.* She lives in Minneapolis.

Maya Marshall is a writer and an editor. She is co-founder of underbellymag.com, the journal on the practical magic of poetic revision. Marshall has earned fellowships from MacDowell, Vermont Studio Center, *Callaloo*, Cave Canem, and the Community of Writers. She works as a manuscript editor for Haymarket Books and serves as a senior editor for *PANK*. Her poems have appeared in *Muzzle Magazine*, *RHINO*, *Potomac Review*, *Blackbird*, and elsewhere.

Max McDonough grew up on the Jersey Shore. His work has previously appeared in *T Magazine*, *Gulf Coast*, *Alaska Quarterly Review*, *Beloit Poetry Journal*, and elsewhere.

John Patrick McShea lives in Pennsylvania. His writing appears or is forthcoming in *Ninth Letter*, *Fence*, *The Journal*, and *TriQuarterly*, among others.

Rachel Morgenstern-Clarren is a poet and translator based out of Montreal. Her work has been honored with an Academy of American Poets Prize, a Hopwood Award, the *Michigan Quarterly Review*'s Page Davidson Clayton Award for Emerging Poets, and a Fulbright Fellowship to Brazil. Her work has recently appeared in *Ninth Letter*, *Ploughshares*, and *Poetry Northwest*. She holds an MFA in poetry and literary translation from Columbia University, and is the Consulate editor for *Joyland Magazine*.

Lena Moses-Schmitt's work appears in *Best New Poets 2015*, *Indiana Review*, *Ninth Letter*, *Cincinnati Review*, *The Normal School*, *Terrain.org*, *Devil's Lake*, and elsewhere. She lives in the Bay Area, where she works as a publicist at Catapult, Soft Skull, and Counterpoint Press.

Skyler Osborne was born in the Midwest. He received an MFA from the Michener Center for Writers in Austin, Texas. His work has most recently appeared in or is forthcoming from *Narrative*, *Colorado Review*, *No Tokens*, *fields*, and *River River*.

ALAN PELAEZ LOPEZ is an Afro-Indigenous writer, collage, and adornment artist from Oaxaca, México. Their work has been nominated for the Pushcart Prize and *Best of the Net*, and has been published in *Poetry*, *Best American Experimental Writing*, *Everyday Feminism*, and elsewhere. They are the author of *Intergalactic Travels: poems from a fugitive alien* (The Operating System Press, 2020).

CHARLIE PECK is from Omaha, Nebraska. He received his MFA from Purdue where he served as editor-in-chief of *Sycamore Review*. He currently teaches at the University of Freiburg in Germany.

KEVIN PHAN is a Vietnamese-American graduate of the University of Michigan with an MFA in creative writing in 2013 and from the University of Iowa with a BA in English literature in 2005. His work has previously appeared in the *Georgia Review*, *Gulf Coast*, *Pleiades*, *Colorado Review*, *Columbia Review*, *Notre Dame Review*, and many other journals. His first full length collection is due out in the fall 2020 from Colorado University Press.

ÖSEL JESSICA PLANTE's fiction and poetry have appeared in *Best New Poets 2017*, *Best Small Fictions 2016*, *Blackbird*, *Narrative*, and *Passages North*, among others. She is winner of the 2018 *Meridian* Editors' Prize in Poetry and is a former fellow of the Vermont Studio Center. She holds an MA in English from the University of North Texas, an MFA from the University of North Carolina at Greensboro, and a PhD from Florida State University. Her first collection of poetry, *Waveland*, is forthcoming from Black Lawrence Press in 2021. She lives in Portland, Oregon.

LIAM POWELL is a writer living in Brooklyn. His poems have been featured or are forthcoming in *Prelude*, *Fields*, *Maggy*, *The Indianapolis Review*, and other publications. He was a semi-finalist for the 2017 Boston Review Discovery prize and is a graduate of Columbia University's School of the Arts.

Joy Priest is the author of *Horsepower* (University of Pittsburgh Press, 2020), winner of the Donald Hall Prize for Poetry from AWP. Her poems have appeared in *Callaloo*, *Gulf Coast*, *Four Way Review*, *Mississippi Review*, *The Rumpus*, *The Breakbeat Poets*, and *Best New Poets 2014* and *2016*, among others. The winner of the 2019 Gearhart Poetry Prize from *The Southeast Review*, she has received fellowships and support from The Frost Place, Bread Loaf Writers' Conference, and the Hurston/Wright Foundation. Currently, she is a 2019–2020 Fine Arts Work Center Fellow in Poetry.

Molly Bess Rector lives in Fayetteville, Arkansas, where she co-curates the Open Mouth Reading Series, a community-based poetry series that hosts monthly readings by visiting writers, as well as workshops and retreats. Molly earned her MFA in poetry from the University of Arkansas. She is the recipient of residencies from the Edward F. Albee Foundation and the Vermont Studio Center, and she served as the inaugural poetry editor for *The Arkansas International*. Molly has also been awarded a grant by Artists 360 to write poems exploring the human elements of nuclear technology.

Aidan Ryan is a writer and co-founder Foundlings Press. He graduated from the Canisius College Creative Writing Program and went on to study at the W.B. Yeats International Summer School in Sligo, Ireland, and to earn his master's in US literature at the University of Edinburgh. He is the author of the cut-up poetry collection *Organizing Isolation: Half-Lives of Love at Long Distance* (Linoleum Press, 2017), and *Hearers and Hearteners* (Canisius College, 2019), a book-length essay on contemporary Irish literature through the lens of the Hassett Family Reading Series. Aidan's fiction and poetry have appeared *in Xavier Review*, *Slipstream*, and *Peach Mag*, among others. He has published essays and interviews with CNN, *The White Review*, *Rain Taxi*, and *Traffic East*, and he is a regular music critic and cultural essayist for *The Skinny*. As an editor, he conceived and managed the production of *My Next Heart: New Buffalo*

Poetry (BlazeVOX, 2017), and with Max Crinnin curated and co-edited the seminal and celebrated *Constant Stranger: After Frank Stanford* (Foundlings Press, 2018). He lives in Buffalo, New York.

SHANNON SANKEY is the author of *We Ran Rapturous*, a winner of *The Atlas Review* 2019 Chapbook Series. Her poems have appeared at *Poets. org*, *Glass: A Journal of Poetry*, *minnesota review*, *Puerto del Sol*, *Sugar House Review*, *Barrelhouse*, and elsewhere. She is the recipient of a 2017 Academy of American Poets University and College Prize and a 2019 SAFTA residency. She holds an MFA from Chatham University, where she was the Whitford Fellow.

XIAO YUE SHAN is a poet born in Dongying, China, and living in Tokyo, Japan. Her chapbook, *How Often I Have Chosen Love*, was published in the spring of 2019. She currently works with *Spittoon Literary Magazine*, *Tokyo Poetry Journal*, and *Asymptote Journal*.

KELLY GRACE THOMAS is the winner of the 2017 Neil Postman Award for Metaphor from *Rattle*, a 2018 finalist for the Rita Dove Poetry Award, a two-time Pushcart Prize nominee, and a *Best of the Net* nominee. *Boat Burned*, her first full-length collection, is forthcoming from YesYes Books in January 2020. Kelly's poems have appeared or are forthcoming in *The Los Angeles Review*, *Redivider*, *Nashville Review*, *Muzzle Magazine*, *DIAGRAM*, *Glass*, and more. Kelly is the education and pedagogy advisor for Get Lit-Words Ignite, a youth poetry nonprofit. She is the co-author of *Words Ignite: Explore, Write, and Perform Classic and Spoken Word Poetry* (Literary Riot). Kelly is also a screenwriter and novelist. She lives in the Bay Area with her husband, Omid. Her website is kellygracethomas.com

ANNIE VIRGINIA is a poetry MFA candidate at the New Writers Project at the University of Texas at Austin. She has her BA in poetry from Sarah Lawrence College. She has taught English to high schoolers, relationship abuse prevention to middle schoolers, and is now teaching American literature to college students. Annie Virginia's work may be found in *The Dead Mule School of Southern Literature, The Legendary, The Literary Bohemian, Cactus Heart, TQ Review, decomP,* and *Seventh Wave,* as well as in the anthologies *The Queer South* and *A Shadow Map: An Anthology by Survivors of Sexual Assault.* Her work was nominated for a Pushcart Prize, was a semifinalist in the 2018 Crab Creek Review Poetry Prize, a semifinalist in the 2018 Red Wheelbarrow Poetry Prize, and was longlisted for the 2019 National Poetry Competition. She was awarded the 2018 Rita Dove Poetry Prize by the Center for Women Writers. This year, she was awarded fellowships from Brooklyn Poets and Writers in Paradise.

A graduate of the Iowa Writers' Workshop, DEVON WALKER-FIGUEROA's poems have appeared or are forthcoming in *The Nation, Poetry, The American Poetry Review, Ploughshares, The Harvard Advocate,* and *The New England Review.* She teaches poetry at University of the Arts in Philadelphia and co-edits Horsethief Books.

JIHYUN YUN is a Korean-American writer from the Bay Area. A Fulbright Research Fellow, she received her BA from UC Davis and an MFA from New York University. She is a winner of The Prairie Schooner Book Prize in Poetry, and her debut full-length collection *Some Are Always Hungry* is forthcoming in September 2020 from University of Nebraska Press. Her work has appeared in *Narrative, Adroit Journal, Poetry Northwest,* and elsewhere.

Participating Magazines

32 Poems
32poems.com

The Account
theaccountmagazine.com

The Adroit Journal
theadroitjournal.org

AGNI Magazine
bu.edu/agni

American Literary Review
americanliteraryreview.com

Anomaly
anmly.org

The Antioch Review
review.antiochcollege.edu

Apple Valley Review
applevalleyreview.com

apt
apt.aforementionedproductions.com

ARTS & LETTERS
artsandletters.gcsu.edu

Atlanta Review
atlantareview.com

Atticus Review
atticusreview.org

The Believer
believermag.com

Bellevue Literary Review
blr.med.nyu.edu

Bellingham Review
bhreview.org

Beloit Poetry Journal
bpj.org

Bennington Review
benningtonreview.org

Better Than Starbucks
betterthanstarbucks.org

Birdfeast
birdfeastmagazine.com

Birmingham Poetry Review
uab.edu/cas/englishpublications/
    birmingham-poetry-review

Blackbird
blackbird.vcu.edu

Blood Orange Review
bloodorangereview.com

Bloodroot
bloodrootlit.org

Blue Mesa Review
bmr.unm.edu

The Boiler Journal
theboilerjournal.com

Boulevard
boulevardmagazine.org

Boxcar Poetry Review
boxcarpoetry.com

cahoodaloodaling
cahoodaloodaling.com

The Carolina Quarterly
thecarolinaquarterly.com

Carve Magazine
carvezine.com

Cascadia Rising Review
cascadiarisingreview.com

Cave Wall
cavewallpress.com

Cherry Tree
washcoll.edu/cherrytree

Cincinnati Review
cincinnatireview.com

Coal Hill Review
coalhillreview.com

The Collagist
thecollagist.com

Connotation Press
connotationpress.com

Copper Nickel
copper-nickel.org

Crazyhorse
crazyhorse.cofc.edu

Cream City Review
creamcityreview.org

Cumberland River Review
crr.trevecca.edu

Cutthroat
cutthroatmag.com

Diode
diodepoetry.com

Ecotone
ecotonemagazine.org

EVENT Magazine
eventmagazine.ca

Fairy Tale Review
fairytalereview.com

Fjords Review
fjordsreview.com

Foglifter
foglifterjournal.com

Foothill: A Journal of Poetry
cgu.edu/foothill

Foundry
foundryjournal.com

The Fourth River
thefourthriver.com

The Georgia Review
thegeorgiareview.com

The Gettysburg Review
gettysburgreview.com

Gingerbread House
gingerbreadhouselitmag.com

Glass: A Journal of Poetry
glass-poetry.com/journal.html

Greensboro Review
greensbororeview.org

Grist: A Journal of the Literary Arts
gristjournal.com

Guernica
guernicamag.com

Hamilton Arts & Letters
HALmagazine.com

Harvard Review
harvardreview.org

Hayden's Ferry Review
haydensferryreview.com

After Happy Hour Review
afterhappyhourreview.com

Image
imagejournal.org

IthacaLit
ithacalit.com

Jabberwock Review
jabberwock.org.msstate.edu

Jet Fuel Review
jetfuelreview.com

The Journal
english.osu.edu/mfa

Juked
juked.com

Kenyon Review
kenyonreview.org

The Lascaux Review
lascauxreview.com

Lunch Ticket
lunchticket.org

Malahat Review
malahatreview.ca

Massachusetts Review
massreview.org

Matador Review
matadorreview.com

*Memorious: A Journal of New Verse
& Fiction*
memorious.org

Michigan Quarterly Review
sites.lsa.umich.edu/mqr

Mid-American Review
casit.bgsu.edu/midamericanreview

the minnesota review
minnesotareview.dukejournals.org

Mississippi Review
sites.usm.edu/mississippi-review

MORIA Literary Magazine
moriaonline.com

Muzzle Magazine
muzzlemagazine.com

The Nashville Review
as.vanderbilt.edu/nashvillereview

Naugatuck River Review
naugatuckriverreview.com

New England Review
nereview.com

Newfound
newfound.org

New Ohio Review
ohio.edu/nor

New Orleans Review
neworleansreview.org

NightBlock
\www.nightblockmag.com

Nimrod International Journal
utulsa.edu/nimrod

Pacifica Literary Review
pacificareview.com

Passages North
passagesnorth.com

Pembroke Magazine
pembrokemagazine.com

Penn Review
pennreview.org

Pigeon Pages
pigeonpagesnyc.com

Ploughshares
pshares.org

Poet Lore
poetlore.com

Poetry
poetrymagazine.org

The Poet's Billow
thepoetsbillow.org

Pretty Owl Poetry
prettyowlpoetry.com

Priestess & Hierophant Presents
priestessandhierophant.com

Psaltery & Lyre
psalteryandlyre.org

Puerto del Sol
puertodelsol.org

Quarterly West
quarterlywest.com

Radar Poetry
radarpoetry.com

Raleigh Review
RaleighReview.org

Rascal
rascaljournal.com

Rat's Ass Review
ratsassreview.net

Redivider
redividerjournal.org

River Styx
riverstyx.org

Roanoke Review
roanokereview.org

Ruminate Magazine
ruminatemagazine.com

Salamander
salamandermag.org

The Shallow Ends
theshallowends.com

Shenandoah
shenandoahliterary.org

Slippery Elm
slipperyelm.findlay.edu

The Southeast Review
southeastreview.org

Southern Indiana Review
usi.edu/sir

The Southern Review
thesouthernreview.org

Spillway
spillway.org

Split Lip
splitlipmagazine.com

Split Rock Review
splitrockreview.org

Sugar House Review
SugarHouseReview.com

Sundog Lit
sundoglit.com

SWWIM Every Day
swwim.org

Sycamore Review
sycamorereview.com

Tahoma Literary Review
tahomaliteraryreview.com

Territory
themapisnot.com

Thrush Poetry Journal
thrushpoetryjournal.com

Tinderbox Poetry Journal
tinderboxpoetry.com

TRACK//FOUR
trackfourjournal.com

Up North Lit
upnorthlit.org

upstreet
upstreet-mag.org

Up the Staircase Quarterly
upthestaircase.org

Virginia Quarterly Review
vqronline.org

Washington Square Review
washingtonsquarereview.com

Waxwing Literary Journal
waxwingmag.org

Whale Road Review
whaleroadreview.com

wildness
readwildness.com

Willow Springs
willowspringsmagazine.org

Winter Tangerine
wintertangerine.com

Zone 3
zone3press.com

Participating Programs

American University Creative Writing Program
american.edu/cas/literature/mfa

Creighton University MFA in Creative Writing
creighton.edu/program/creative-writing-mfa

Florida International University MFA in Creative Writing
english.fiu.edu/creative-writing

Florida State University Creative Writing
english.fsu.edu/programs/creative-writing

Hollins University Jackson Center for Creative Writing
hollinsmfa.wordpress.com

Kansas State University MFA in Creative Writing Program
k-state.edu/english/programs/cw

McNeese State University MFA Program
mfa.mcneese.edu

Miami Univerisity Creative Writing MFA
miamioh.edu/cas/academics/departments/english/academics/
    graduate-studies/creative-writing/residential-mfa

Minnesota State University Mankato Creative Writing Program
english.mnsu.edu/cw/index.html

Monmouth University Creative Writing
monmouth.edu/school-of-humanities-social-sciences/ma-english.aspx

Mount Saint Mary's University MFA in Creative Writing
msmu.edu/creativewriting

New Mexico Highlands University MA in English (Creative Writing)
nmhu.edu/current-students/graduate/arts-and-sciences/english

New School Writing Program
newschool.edu/writing

New York University Creative Writing Program
as.nyu.edu/cwp

North Carolina State MFA in Creative Writing
english.chass.ncsu.edu/graduate/mfa

Northwestern University MA/MFA in Creative Writing
sps.northwestern.edu/program-areas/graduate/creative-writing

The Ohio State University MFA Program in Creative Writing
english.osu.edu/mfa

Ohio University Creative Writing PhD
ohio.edu/cas/english/grad/creative-writing/index.cfm

Pacific University Master of Fine Arts in Writing
pacificu.edu/as/mfa

San Diego State University MFA in Creative Writing
mfa.sdsu.edu

Sarah Lawrence College MFA in Writing
sarahlawrence.edu/writing-mfa

Syracuse University MFA in Creative Writing
english.syr.edu/cw/cw-program.html

Texas Tech University Creative Writing Program
depts.ttu.edu/english/cw

UMass Amherst MFA for Poets and Writers
umass.edu/englishmfa

UMass Boston MFA Program in Creative Writing
umb.edu/academics/cla/english/grad/mfa

University of Alabama at Birmingham Graduate Theme in Creative Writing
uab.edu/cas/english/graduate-program/creative-writing

University of Connecticut Creative Writing Program
creativewriting.uconn.edu

University of Idaho MFA in Creative Writing
uidaho.edu/class/english/graduate/mfa-creative-writing

University of Illinois at Chicago Program for Writers
engl.uic.edu/CW

University of Kansas Graduate Creative Writing Program
englishcw.ku.edu

University of Maryland MFA Program
english.umd.edu

University of Mississippi MFA in Creative Writing
mfaenglish.olemiss.edu

University of New Orleans Creative Writing Workshop
uno.edu/writing

University of North Texas Creative Writing
english.unt.edu/creative-writing-0

University of South Florida MFA in Creative Writing
english.usf.edu/graduate/concentrations/cw/degrees

University of Texas Michener Center for Writers
michener.utexas.edu

University of Utah Creative Writing MFA
english.utah.edu

University of South Florida Creative Writing
english.usf.edu/graduate/concentrations/cw/degrees/

Vermont College of Fine Arts MFA in Writing
vcfa.edu

Virginia Tech MFA in Creative Writing Program
liberalarts.vt.edu/academics/graduate-programs/masters-programs/
    master-of-fine-arts-in-creative-writing.html

Western Michigan University Creative Writing Program
wmich.edu/english

West Virginia University MFA Program
creativewriting.wvu.edu

The series editor wishes to thank the many poets involved in our first round of reading:

Kate Coleman, Emily Lawson, Emily Nason, Caleb Nolen, Aimee Seu, Sean Shearer, and Sasha Prevost.

Special thanks to Jason Coleman and the University of Virginia Press for editorial advice and support.